MW01264231

Daughter of the Sandhills

by

A. Louise Hill

DORRANCE
PUBLISHING CO
EST. 1920
PITTSBURGH, PENNSYLVANIA 15238

The contents of this work, including, but not limited to, the accuracy of events, people, and places depicted; opinions expressed; permission to use previously published materials included; and any advice given or actions advocated are solely the responsibility of the author, who assumes all liability for said work and indemnifies the publisher against any claims stemming from publication of the work.

Dorrance Publishing Co
585 Alpha Drive
Suite 103
Pittsburgh, PA 15238
Visit our website at *www.dorrancebookstore.com*

ISBN: 978-1-4809-2499-4
eISBN: 978-1-4809-2269-3

Table of Contents

Chapter 6 — Hard Work

Preface

This book contains a history in poetry form of the Vath and Williams family, as Helen L. Vath (my mother) and Walter L. Williams (my father) merged their lives through marriage. They were born and lived in the Sandhills of Nebraska all their lives. Their parents were truly pioneers and this book reflects this family's struggles, hard work and simple joys, as they reared their children on this small ranch. The ranch was located in the southern part of Arthur County, Nebraska in the heart of the Nebraska Sandhills. Their history in poetry form covers from the early 1900's until the late 1960's.

My mother, Helen L. Vath Williams, was a rural schoolteacher and during my seventh and eighth grade years, she taught me the fundamentals of writing poetry. Thus, we have this book of poetry about their pioneer lives.

May this book preserve the history of a way of life that is now gone. My desire is that those who read this book will not only enjoy the simple poetry, but will be thankful for all the conveniences we now have.

—A. Louise Hill

Notes of Dedication and Appreciation

I would like to dedicate this book to my deceased husband, William B. Hill. It was his vision that one day I would put these poems into book form for others to enjoy.

I would like to thank my daughters, Deborah and Terresa, for encouraging me as each poem was written. It is their history as well, and for Deborah who did the illustrations. A special thanks to Deborah and Neil for providing a place of quiet and peace so I could concentrate and put this book together.

Finally, I also want to thank my friend, Rachel Harvoy, who did the typing of the manuscript; and to all my friends who gave advice and encouragement. Without all the above, I may not have written it.

Chapter 1
Family

Arthur County Pioneers

In a covered wagon
My grandparents came
To settle the land
On their homestead claim.

They had a team of horses
And a couple of cows.
They found their section
But I don't know how.

The land had been surveyed
But all the hills looked the same.
Still Grandpa found his way
To his homestead claim.

There were 640 acres,
'Twas a section he drew.
He'd do the best with it
That he could do.

He had to "prove up"
For he now owned the land
And he would do this
With his own two hands.

In the covered wagon
They did reside
Until they built a "soddy"
And could move inside.

My grandmother was a city gal
And unaccustomed to this life
That she would live,
As Jesse Vath's wife.

Together they labored
And shed many tears,
`Cause times were hard.
In those long ago years.

They raised a family
And improved their land.
The farm turned out better
Than what they had planned.

My grandparents are now
Long dead and gone
And to our family
Their land no longer belongs.

When I drive to their section,
I see their sweat, blood and tears
That they invested in the land,
As Arthur County pioneers.

2-01-05

'The Fence Post, Plains Edition, March 11, 2006

Days of Prohibition

A way back then
In the time of prohibition
For a drink of alcohol
My grandpa got to wishin'.

Where would he find
Those who had booze?
To pursue this quest
He then did choose.

He heard there were those
At Birdwood Creek
Who had the goods
That he did seek.

He had to approach
These men with care.
Because booze was illegal.
He was aware

That these men were shifty
And had hidden guns.
He carefully approached
These dangerous ones.

He went alone,
When it was almost night.
He did admit
He was filled with fright.
He had heard by the grapevine

A still was there.
Of his approaching presence
He knew they were aware.

From behind a clump of bushes
Two men came,
As he greeted them
And told them his name,

A deal was made
For a jug of moonshine.
Up to this point
He was doing fine.

As he went back to his pickup
Hidden over the hill,
He stumbled and fell
And all the booze he did spill.

Fear of these men
He now did feel
And was afraid to go back
To make another deal.

When men grew thirsty
And for a drink was wishin',
This is what some did
In the days of prohibition.
1-29-05

[2]The Fence Post, Plains Edition, September 24, 2005

Doctor Grandpa

Pitching manure
Out of the barn
Is one thing you did,
If you lived on a farm.

The pitchfork Dad used
Had only four prongs.
I'll tell of a time,
When things went wrong.

Dad was busy
Pitching out the manure.
Remember each load
Was never pure.

Down came the pitchfork
Into Dad's calf.
He grimaced with pain.
He did not laugh.

With all of his might
He pulled the prong out.
"I need a doctor,"
Dad wanted to shout.

"I'll be your doctor,"
Grandpa said to my dad.
"I'll be the best doctor
That you've ever had."

They went to the house
To get Grandpa's supplies.
If infection set in,
My dad could die.

A baby syringe
Is what Grandpa took.
With peroxide he filled it.
(Don't give me that look.)

He wiped off the wound,
Placed the syringe there and squeezed
The terrible pain
Brought Dad to his knees.

The peroxide did bubble
And it turned to foam.
By Grandpa the doctor
Dad was doctored at home.

Grandpa then said,
"I'm not yet through.
There's still one more thing
That I know to do."

He took the syringe
Filled it with iodine.
At this point in the procedure
Dad was not doing fine.

Grandpa placed the syringe
In the wound and did squeeze.

Great pain it caused
But Grandpa was pleased.

A week went by
And then another.
No red streaks appeared
Neath Dad's bandage cover.

The wound healed completely.
Is what I saw
And this was because
We had a doctor Grandpa.
6-20-03

[3]Nebraska Fence Post, February 7, 2004

Mother's Hands

When I was a child,
Please understand,
The most beautiful thing
Was my mother's hands.

I watched them carefully
Stitch and sew
To make new clothes
So I proudly could go

To school every day
And not be ashamed.
In watching her hands
New insight I gained

Of what was important
By the things she did.
The love in her hands
Was never hid.

I watched her hands
Knead bread for a meal.
To have extras for dinner
Was no big deal.

Her hands did the things
A farm wife should.
We depended on them
Because we knew we could.

Her hands on by brow,
When I was ill,
Comforted me
And helped me be still.

With her hands she would shoo me
Off to bed.
To strike me in anger
She never was led.

The smell of food
Was oft' on her hands
And this brought me comfort
Please understand.

I'd watch her hands
Play the old violin
Though fame and fortune
She never did win.

The best example of love,
Please understand
Was the love I found
In my mother's hands.

11-22-04

[4] The Fence Post, Plains Edition, May 7, 2005

Grandma's Table

There she was
Standing out from the wall.
She was thirty-nine inches
Which was not very tall.

She had four legs
Coming up from the floor.
She had two leaves
To make room for more.

Children — adult —
Relative or friend
Welcome one and all
Was the message she'd send.

Across her back
And oilcloth was laid.
Come eat with me
Was the statement she made.

I can see her still
With hot steamy dishes.
I can taste of her food
Which was always delicious.

Each person would come
With a big appetite.
To gather together
Was quite a delight.

She took great pleasure
In listening to the chatter.

If more than one talked
It really didn't matter.

There was more to her
Than being made of wood
For at Grandma's table
I then understood

And I knew I was loved
By a large fam-i-ly.
That's what Grandma's table
Showed to me.

We still all come
Maybe once a year
To gather around
And experience the cheer

That Grandma's table
Brings to each one.
We'll always remember
The laughter and fun.

Come one and all
If you are able
And enjoy a time
At Grandma's table.

Grandma's table!

8-11-01

[5]Nebraska Fence Post, December 15, 2001

Oven Door Seat

On a cold winter morning
And I was snug in bed,
To get out of my warm nest
I never once felt led.

From the bottom of the stairs
I'd hear my mother call,
"It's time to get up."
Still I'd snuggle with my doll.

From underneath the covers
I'd stick my one foot out.
"I'm getting up, Mother,"
At her I did shout.

I'd stomp my foot once or twice
And put it back in bed
To get out in the freezing room
I certainly was not led.

I'd lie there feeling guilty
`Cause Mom I had deceived.
This way of delaying getting up
In my head I had conceived.

The smell of fresh fried bacon
Drifted up the stairs.
That I was really hungry
I suddenly was aware.

I quickly jumped out of bed
And dress in my cold clothes.
I didn't stop to put on shoes
Though I now had icy toes.

The first place I would head
Was for the oven door,
Where I could sit and warm up.
Now who could ask for more?

With three more calls my brothers
Would descend the flight of stairs.
That now I had the oven door seat
My brothers were aware.

If you've never slept in a freezing room
Without any speck of heat,
Then you can't begin to imagine
How welcome was an oven door seat.

11-13-04

Sandhills Water

As I came from the field,
I was oh, so dry.
Give me a drink
Quick, before I die.

I went to the pump
Standing in the yard.
I began to pump
And I pumped so hard

`Till up from its depth
Gushed a cool, clear stream.
It brought me to reality
And out of a dream.

I bent down to the stream
And it splashed in my face.
I caught some in my hand.
What a wonderful taste!

This water was as pure,
As any water could be.
'Twas Sandhills water
And it was free.

It was oh, so cold
And had a sweet taste.
Not one drop in my hand
Did I want to waste.

Today in the stores
Water is sold
In plastic bottles
And it's not very cold.

When I'm real thirsty
I long to go
To the pump in the yard
Of so long ago.

Today's water in bottles
Is not the same thing
As the water from the pump
Of which I dream.

Cool! Clear!
Sandhills water.

1-28-02

The Sandhills, My Home

Buffalo and Indians
Long ago did roam
Across the place
That I now call home.

Pony Express riders
Once raced by
Under the hot, hot
Clear Nebraska sky.

Stage-coaches stopped rolling
Progress was being made,
When across the prairie
Steel tracks were laid.

With smoke from engines
And the whistles of the trains
Hordes of settlers and families
To the Sandhills came.

Some came in covered wagons
And others on horseback
But they all came to settle
Their various land tracts.

Dugouts were built
And sod houses were made,
While plans for the towns
Were then being laid.

Sturdy, barbed wire fences
Were quickly being built.
The land was being tamed
For which no one felt guilt.

Though winter blizzards raged
O'er valleys and hills
And plagues of grasshoppers came
The settlers remained still.

You see Sandhill people
Are a sturdy folk.
While some did prosper
Others went broke.

The Sandhills of Nebraska,
Are as we know it today,
Because the price for a new life.
These settlers did pay.

`Tis the land where the Indians
And buffalos once roamed
I'll always call these Nebraska
Sandhills my home.

9-25-05

⁶The Fence Post, Plains Edition, April 1, 2006

Boots as a Friend

The grandparents took Debbie shopping,
When she was but four.
She had a big smile,
As she returned through the door.

They had been shopping
A wardrobe to complete
But her favorite things
Were the boots on her feet.

A dress with fringe
And a belt at her waist
Were nothing compared
To the boots of her taste.

They were made of real leather
And had a high heel.
The grandparents had bought them
 At such a good deal.

It was love at first sight,
When they did shop.
They were brown at the bottom
With red at the top.

Soon it was night
And time for bed.
To take off her boots
Debbie was not led.

I went in to tuck her
Secure for the night
But what I saw
Was a humorous sight.

The sheets were pulled
Clear up to her head
But what she'd done
Was wore her boots to bed.

Some children take teddy bears
To bed at night
But Debbie would just snuggle
Her boots up tight.

Then came the sorrowful,
Tear filled day,
When we gave those cowboy
Boots away.

As we tell of Debbie saying
Goodbye in the end,
You'll be able to identify
If you've had boots as a friend.

8-12-05

[7] The Fence Post, Plains Edition,
February 18, 2006

Chapter 2
Fun

Boys Will Be Boys

Boys will be boys
Or so it's said.
To tell a true story
I now feel led.

Out in the hills
Many years ago.
Two boys met up
With a deadly foe.

They were going down the road
So innocent and free,
When they said to each other,
"Do you see what I see?"

In the pickup lights
In two trails called a road
A black-and-white animal
The headlights showed.

He was just a baby
So he'd do no harm.
"We'll make him a pet
And take him to the farm."

The pickup stopped!
One boy got out
And picked up the animal
And turned about.

He and the animal
Got back in the cab.
A baby skunk
Is what they had.

"He's too little to squirt,"
Said Larry at the wheel.
Oh what pleasure
These boys did feel!

The tail Edward lifted
And the skunk did squirt,
All over the boys,
The cab and their shirts.

Skunk perfume
Is what they wore,
When they came home
Through the farmhouse door.

They learned a lesson
From the skunk that day.
Boys will be boys
But with skunks don't play.

12-18-02

[8] Nebraska Fence Post, February 15, 2003

Fishing the Old Way

"Fishy, fishy,
In the lake
Come and take
My fishing bait."

This is a rhyme
I often said,
When to go fishing
We were led.

I always used
An old cane pole
When to the fishing
Hole we'd go.

It had a line
Where we added a weight.
A bright red bobber
We did take

And placed it above
Where we put two hooks.
A big fat worm
We finally took

To use as bait
To catch a fish.
For a sunny day
We all did wish.

We'd throw the line out
And watch the bobber,

Where it floated
On the water.

When the bobber went under,
We jerked with our might
And landed a fish
To our delight.

My cousin one day
Went with me to fish.
To catch a fish
Is what she wished.

With her line in the water
She sat on the bank
As I caught fish,
Her spirits sank.

Would she catch a fish
She began to wonder
But after an hour
Her bobber went under.

When she caught that fish,
This is what she did say,
"It sure took a long time
To get on there today."

Fancy methods of fishing
Today people know
But give to me
My old cane pole.

7-5-03

Bullheads

Yum-yum! Yum-yum!
How good they taste.
These fried bullheads
I cannot waste.

Yes, they have bones
That are fine you see
But I spit them out.
They don't bother me.

When I was a child,
We'd catch a hundred or more,
Fishing seldom from a boat
But usually from shore.

I'd be so excited,
When the bobber went under.
I'd have another fish on,
As sure as thunder.

The Sandhill lakes
Are mostly dry,
Where me, as a child,
Would go and try

To catch some fish
On a sunny day.
I worked hard at fishing
For I didn't come to play.

Some days we caught more.
Some days we caught less
But eating fried bullheads
Is what I liked best.

Those were the days,
When fishing we'd go
But now Sandhill lakes
Are either gone or low.

There's one Sandhill lake
That's pretty close by,
If fishing for bullheads,
You want to try.

Yum-yum! Yum-yum!
We sure are the winner
`Cause we're going to Mom's
To eat bullheads for dinner.

5-10-04

Five in a Bed

When I was but
A wee little girl,
Alone in my bed
I loved to curl.

I'd pile the quilts
Up so high.
I enjoyed my bed
I'll not deny.

How things did change,
When company came.
Alone in my bed
I did not remain.

Four girl cousins
With me did sleep,
Three at the head
And two at the feet.

If you were sleeping
At the foot of the bed,
You usually had feet
Next to your head.

A tug of war
We had with the covers
But we rarely fussed
With one another.

Sleeping alone
Children now are led
But they're missing the fun
Of five in a bed.

8-16-03

[9]Nebraska Fence Post, March 13, 2004

My House in a Tree

Have you ever heard
Of a house in a tree?
When I was a child,
There was one for me.

Each branch became
A different room.
The wind was then
My vacuum broom.

This tree house was found
In the yard of our ranch.
My bedroom was
On an upper branch.

That it had walls
Do not assume
But on the lowest branch
Was the living room.

In this tree house
I would daily climb.
With imaginary friends
I'd spend my time.

One day I pretended
On the sofa to be.
I leaned back
And fell out of the tree.

My breath was gone,
As I hit the ground
But no broken bones
In me were found.

This story is true,
As true as can be,
But don't lean back
If you're in a house in a tree.

2-17-04

My Swimming Pool

On a ranch
What do you do
To make yourself
Oh so cool,

Whene'er the sun
Is so hot?
What as a child
Was my favorite spot?

Well, I would go
And put on shorts
But there were no tennis
Or basketball courts.

So, to the horse tank
I would go.
Its cool refreshment
I would know

As into that tank
I would climb in
To play around
And take a swim.

The moss between
My toes did ooze
Where minutes before
I had shed my shoes.

The water seemed
About three feet deep.
Sometimes I'd struggle
My balance to keep.

The horse tank's sides
Were made of metal.
Around it's circle
I would pedal

And pretend it was
My swimming pool.
It was refreshing.
It kept me cool.

Around the sides
There was a rim.
I'd climb on it
And then jump in.

Oh, what a splash
I would make!
It was my pool
For goodness' sake.

For an hour
I would play
And then jump out
And go my way.

Whene'er I was hot
And wanted to keep cool,

I'd return
To my swimming pool.

2-12-02

[10]Nebraska Fence Post, August 24, 2002

Chewing Gum

When I was little
And had gum to chew,
When bedtime came,
What was I to do?

I could swallow the gum
Or throw it away
But how could I save it
For another day?

There was an answer
Just above my head.
I would put it
On the head of the bed.

The head of the bed
Was made of metal
So I put it there
And into bed I did snuggle.

All night long
I dreamed of my dreams.
I awoke in the morning
To do my own thing.

Soon I remembered
I had gum to chew,
So I rushed to the bed
And you would have too.

The gum was hard,
As it came off of the bed.
To pop it in my mouth
Is how I was led.

Soon it was soft,
As I chewed away.
I was glad to chew it
Another day.

You've never lived
It has been said
Unless you've chewed gum
From the head of the bed.

10-12-03

The Fence Post, Plains Edition, January 13, 2007

Only Eight and Little

One summer day our parents
Went down the road to town.
We were not alone for long
`Cause some neighbors came around.

These neighbors were two boys
About my brother's age.
To have a little fun
They'd simply set the stage.

"Let's get the bigger calves in
That are older than a year.
I want my sis to ride
That biggest Hereford steer."

"But Larry, I'm a girl
And I am only eight."
"You'll do alright, Sis,
If you just sit up straight."

The yearlings soon were gathered
Out behind the barn.
I was reassured
They'd do me no harm.

They somehow held this steer
`Till they got me on his back
They twisted up his tail
And gave his back a whack.

I held on for dear life
To the rope around his middle.
They knew that I'd be dumped
For I was eight and little.

I rode that bucking steer
For quite a little while.
I ruined all their fun
As they lost their smirky smiles.

Soon that old steer
Stopped dead in his track.
I simply dismounted
From my place upon his back.

I always will remember
My legs clamped around the middle
Of that Hereford steer I rode,
When I was eight and little.

6-12-03

[12] Nebraska Fence Post, November 22, 2003

Paraffin Gum

Long ago,
When I was young,
I had a different
Type of chewing gum.

When with my dad
To the dance hall I would go,
I'd be rewarded
With gum I'd know.

Dad would take
A block of paraffin wax
And as a child
I'd always relax

While Dad shaved it on the floor
So the floor would be slick.
In anticipation
My lips I did lick.

I knew from this block
That I would get some
And this would become
My chewing gum.

When I was given
A little to chew,
It fell to pieces
Is what it would do

But I would just keep
Chewing away.
It soon became gum
For me that day.

It was always white
And didn't change colors.
I wasn't chewing alone
`Cause so did my brothers.

This paraffin gum
Had no taste
`Cause it was precious
It I never would waste.

If you put in your mouth.
Something cold to drink,
This gum would separate
Before you could think.

You've never lived
Until you've tried some.
Why not try
Some paraffin gum?

4-15-04

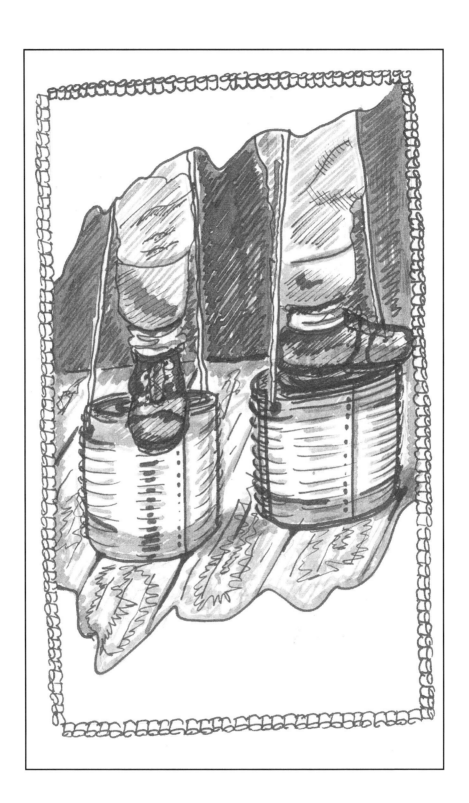

Coffee Can Stilts

The children were excited
For they had a plan.
They decided to make stilts
From some old coffee cans.

Two cans were needed,
One for each shoe.
They laid their plans
As to what they would do.

They needed a nail
To reach their goals.
In the sides of each can
They'd poke two holes.

Then they took cord
Or some heavy string.
Up past their knees
This cord they'd bring

.

Then they'd double
The cord in size.
To have it too short
Was never wise.

The end of the cord
Was placed through each hole.
When inside it was knotted,
They'd reached their goal.

Now for the challenge
Of what they had built.
Could they now walk
On their coffee can stilt?

As they mounted
With each cord held tight,
They tried to walk
But the dust they did bite.

This challenge they took
And finally did win,
As they walked to the cellar
And back again.

Children show excitement,
When things they have built,
Even such things
As coffee can stilts.

1-30-03

[13] Nebraska Fence Post, July 26, 2003

Crash and Burn

Out the door
One cold winter day
Went my brothers and I
In the snow to play.

We were bundled up
From our head to our toes.
Our destination
Everyone knows

Was the biggest hill
Just west of our home.
All over the face
Of this hill we would roam.

We each took turns
Pulling the sled.
We all were thinking
Of the fun ahead.

We huffed and panted,
As we climbed the hill.
To ride the sled down
Would be a great thrill.

When we reached the top,
We all climbed aboard
Then down the hill
On the sled we soared.

I was in front
And my feet were to guide
The path of the sled.
I was filled with pride.

We were doing fine
Heading down the hill,
With me at the helm
We'd not take a spill.

I looked to the side
And was distracted instead.
I didn't see
What was dead ahead.

There before us
Were several soapweeds.
The voices of my brothers
I tried to heed.

Before I could adjust
Or make a turn
We three had hit them
And had crashed and burned.

Larry and Gerald
Flew off of the sled.
I flew off
Landing on my head.

The sled continued
On down the hill,

As we recovered
From that nasty spill.

Sometimes down the hill
We'd ride all the way
We had such fun
That winter day.

How about you?
Would you like to go
And play with us
If you have snow?

2-19-03

[14] Nebraska Fence Post, March 15, 2003

King of the Mountain

Who would like
To be crowned king
And for the happiness
It would bring?

I'll tell the story
Of one small boy
Who experienced
Such a joy.

To become king of the mountain
Is what they'd play,
When the cousins came
To the ranch that day.

They'd all go out
Behind the barn,
Where they could play
And do no harm.

The haystacks were there
All in a line.
They beckoned the children
To come and climb

Up the sides
The top to gain.
If one fell down,
No one complained.

The first to make it
Up topside
Would yell to the others
With all his pride,

"I'm king of the mountain
Don't you see.
Just come on and try
To topple me."

Hands were trying
To grab his shirt
To make him fall
And hit the dirt.

The littlest one grabbed
A hold of a shoe
The king was toppled
Then he was through.

The little one scrambled
Up to the top.
Now he was king
All others he'd stop.

He was youngest
But he was quick.
Off the hay mountain
Others he'd kick.

The bigger kids
Didn't want him to play

`Til he became king
Of the mountain that day.

From this there's a lesson
That all can learn.
Even the littlest one
No one should spurn.

For he may be one
On life's haystack
Who'll stay on the top,
When others fall back.

Are you on some mountain
In work or in play?
Keep trying for you
Might be king someday!

11-17-02

Snipe Hunting

Want to go hunting
Anyone?
Have you tried hunting
Without a gun?

One day to Grandpa's
A city cousin came.
The grownups decided
To play this game.

Snipe hunting is what
They decided to play.
It was done at night
And never in day.

She was told snipes
Would come into her bag,
If she held it just right
And didn't let it sag.

This hunting could be done
Only on a moonless night
For snipes had extremely
Good eyesight.

They left her alone
Out in a field
And to their instruction
She was to yield.

They thought she was
Entirely in their power,
As they drove around
For about one half hour.

They went to the house
To laugh up their sleeve
About the cousin
They were able to deceive.

When they went into
My grandpa's house,
Who was sitting there
Quiet as a mouse?

There the city cousin
Sat with her bag
For someone had told her
Of this snipe hunting gag.

People aren't as naive,
As they appear to be.
The one who told her
Was none other but me.

12-14-04

Summer Ice Cream

What did we do
When the days were hot
And there was no
Air conditioned spot?

We as a family
Decided to make
Homemade ice cream
And chocolate cake.

The cake was Mother's
Thing to do.
The recipe for ice cream
The entire family knew.

You take milk and cream
Then beat in the eggs.
To add the sugar
I often did beg.

A dash of salt
And vanilla too
Was added last.
Now what did we do?

Mother was the expert
Chocolate cake baker
While we got out
The ice cream maker.

In the middle was
A metal container
Where the ice cream would form
Much, much later.

First into it
The mixture we'd pour,
Insert the paddles
Where they were before

We closed the lid
And attached the crank.
We placed around it
A chipped ice bank.

After adding rock salt
We began to turn
And after some time
We began to yearn

For someone else
To take our place.
We couldn't stop
Or slacken our pace.

At last the crank
Began turning quite slow.
The ice cream was made
We now did know.

We removed the crank
And took off the lid.
There in the container
The ice cream was hid.

To describe the taste
What do I say
`Bout the taste of ice cream
On a hot summer day?

7-4-03

Spotted Horse Hall

It's Saturday night
At old Spotted Horse Hall.
It soon would hold dancers
Wall to wall.

Off in the car
Our family would go
To prepare the hall
For the "do-si-do."

A block of wax
Would be chipped on the floor
To make it slicker
Than it was before.

We kids would slide
And have great fun
On the dance floor
Before the dance had begun.

Dad would pump up
The white gas lanterns.
The shadows they gave off
Formed many patterns.

In back of the hall
A small kitchen was there.
The odor of brewed coffee
Filled the air.

Opposite the kitchen
Wooden bunks had been made
Where sleepy children
That night could be laid.

Before long
The band would arrive.
Sometimes its members
Were as many as five.

People would come
From near and far.
There might be a whole bunch
Just stacked in one car.

From the benches along
The sides of the hall
"Come dance with me,"
Was the gentlemen's call.

Waltz and schottische,
And square dance too
Were some of the dances
They would do.

I fondly recall
Dancing with my dad.
Oh, what fun,
As a child I had.

They'd take a break
In the middle of the night.

A big fat hot dog
Was my delight.

When the dance was over,
We were the last to go home.
This is the end
Of this Spotted Horse poem.

1-5-04

[15] The Fence Post, Plains Edition, September 9, 2006

The Box Supper

I remember now
Many years ago
To a box supper
I was to go.

The women and girls
Would prepare a box
And try to be
Sly as a fox

By decorating it
In some secret place
And filling it with
Things good to taste.

For no one should know
Which box was mine,
When it became
Auction time.

The women's boxes
Were set apart.
I recognized Mother's
Right from the start.

As the auction began,
There were bids by the men
On the most pretty box
They hoped to win.

Soon it was time
For the boys to bid
On the girls' boxes
Where each lunch was hid.

They picked up one
And it sold right away.
They picked up mine.
Will it sell today?

When the bidding began
There were bidders true blue.
As the bidding grew higher
Some dropped out too.

Now there were only
Two boys that kept bidding.
They kept on going
And were not kidding

That they'd win the box
That was so pretty to see.
They didn't know
It was made by me.

At last one boy
Ran out of dough.
Who made the box
They soon would know.

When the winning boy
Paid the auctioneer,

I was shy
But I drew near.

"You bought the box
That I have made.
It was a high price
That you have paid."

"Come on," he said.
"Let's eat this chow.
I knew it was yours
But don't ask me how,"

That night's box supper
I'll never forget.
The memory of it
Is with me yet.

6-26-03

[16] The Fence Post, Plains Edition,
March 10, 2007

Daddy, the Bear

When I was little
There was a game we'd play
With our dad
At the end of the day.

He'd get down on all fours
And with a scary face
He'd growl like a bear
And us kids he'd chase.

I'd scream and holler,
When he came near to me.
I'd climb o'er the furniture
To get away scot-free.

He didn't seem to be
My loving dad
`Cause he growled like a bear
And a scary face he had.

Mom always enjoyed
Watching us play.
I'll now tell you
`Bout what happened one day.

Mom was sitting
On the couch carefree.
Dad was chasing
None other but me.

I ran past my mom
With Dad close behind.
Dad had a plan
That was so clever in mind.

He thought he'd show Mom
That he was a bear.
What was about to happen
Mom was not aware.

As he passed by Mom's legs,
He turned and took a bite.
He didn't bite hard.
He only bit light.

She jumped and she hollered.
It caught her by surprise.
Dad hurried away
For he was very wise.

We kids would have laughed,
If we thought we'd dare.
That's how it went
When my daddy played bear.

5-8-04

[17] The Fence Post, Plains Edition, February 10, 2007

The Charivari

A young farm couple
Got married one day.
To keep it a secret
They wanted it to stay.

About two nights
After their wedding night,
I remember long ago
That the moon was bright.

They thought early to bed
And early to rise
But this night they were in
For a big surprise.

About two hours
After going to bed
To look out the window
The bride felt led.

"Honey, there are cars
Coming from everywhere.
Quick, let's put on our clothes
Hanging there on the chair?"

Some people were shouting
And all the horns were honking.
To the outside door
The bride and groom were walking.

The neighbors had come
To honor this pair.
So soon after their wedding
But how would they dare?

What happened next
Was a big surprise.
The groom was kidnapped
By some of the guys.

The bride was shaking
And was so afraid.
What would happen to her husband
Who had been waylaid?

When next she saw him
He was dressed in her clothes
Including a girdle
And old fashioned hose.

A wheelbarrow awaited
This newly wed pair.
The groom was told,
"Drive your bride with care."

Their destination was
The horse tank by the barn.
They never meant
To do them harm.

The destination was reached.
This was all in good fun.

Then the couple brought out
Treats for everyone.

This happened to couples,
When I was but wee,
And it was known,
As a charivari.

5-19-05

[18] The Fence Post, Plains Edition, November 12, 2005

The Great Sandhill

The great Sandhill
`Twas a mile from our home.
On the crest of that hill
And through its bowels we did roam.

When we'd play hide and seek,
What joy it did bring.
We'd roll down its slope
And that sort of thing.

The southern slope
Filled with loose, white sand
Took all of one's skill
At your command

To climb to the top,
A victor to be.
I'll tell of a time
It about swallowed me.

I'd gone to that Sandhill
All alone
To play in the sand
And its cavity to roam.

I dug in the bank
Of hard, dry sand,
The danger of its slope
I didn't understand.

I laid and rolled down
That southern slope.
I forgot that to get out
You might need a rope.

I was at the bottom
And played for a while
I tried to climb out
I then had no smile.

I climbed halfway up
But couldn't go further.
Would I ever see
Again my dear mother?

Each time I'd pull
One foot from the sand,
More sand rolled on me.
 It even covered my hand.

I began to panic.
How would I get out?
No one at home
Could hear my shout.

My heart beat fast
Within my chest.
The sun was setting
Off in the West.

I clawed at the sand
And moved an inch.

I decided to pray
For I was in a pinch.

Instead of standing,
I lay down on the sand,
Then I began crawling.
`Twas a wonderful plan.

With much effort
I reached the top.
Hurried home
And did not stop.

I told no one
Of my ordeal
But respect for that Sandhill
I'd always feel.

I never want again
To have such a thrill
That was given to me
By that great Sandhill.

1-6-02

[19] Nebraska Fence Post, September 28, 2002

The New Lariat

Dad bought a brand-new lariat.
An idea we kids had.
It was a common thing for us
To not consult our dad.

From the barn peg we removed it
And took it to a tree.
A wonderful new rope swing
Is what we kids could see.

Larry shimmied up the tree
And climbed out on a limb.
He took the end of the lariat
And it was secured by him

The lariat was a long one.
It even reached the ground.
With hay a gunnysack was filled.
`Twas the perfect seat we found.

We tied it to the lariat.
It seemed the thing to do.
They wanted to do a test run
So they asked me. "Why not you?"

"Okay," I said, "if you'll push it
Close to the lowest limb."
Then, I scrambled up the tree
And took the rope from them.

With both hands I held it
And jumped right on the sack.
I swung out just like Tarzan.
Confidence I did not lack.

We were having such great fun,
When Dad pulled up in the drive.
Where'd you get that rope," he asked.
The moment of truth arrived.

Sheepishly we answered,
"We found it in the barn
And to use it, Dad, we thought
It would do no harm?"

All four of us kids
Had bottoms that were red.
Instead of an old rope
We'd used Dad's new lariat instead.

To all kids near and far
I have one thing to say,
"Never use your dad's new lariat,
When you want to play."

1-12-04

[20] The Fence Post, Plains Edition,
July 15, 2006

The Ice Skating Party

During the winter
So long ago
To a Sandhill lake
We all would go.

Before we'd leave,
We'd load old tires.
They'd be the fuel
For our nighttime fires.

Our neighbors would form
A caravan.
The ice would be checked
By a grownup man.

When we arrived
At the ice-filled lake,
We'd all put on
A pair of skates.

A fire would be lit
From the old, old tires.
The older women sat
Around the fires,

While Dad and the men
Would pull on a sled
All the little children.
How fast they sped.

On a scoop shovel
I'd sometimes ride.
At times it was scary
I must confide.

There was a woman
Who wanted to skate.
Where to tie the pillows
She did debate.

She thought they'd cushion
Her, if she fell.
She started out
And did quite well.

Then all of a sudden
She hit the ice.
Where she fell
Was not very nice.

She hit her head
For no pillow was there.
No longer for skating
Did she care.

Marshmallows we'd roast
Over the fire.
Then back to the cars
We'd all retire.

On the way home
The kids would sleep

Underneath the quilts
In the backseat.

I still can remember
The people so hardy
That attended the nightly
Ice skating party.

2-20-04

[21] Nebraska. Fence Post, February 12, 2005

The Picture Show

On Saturdays as a girl,
To the movies I would go
We didn't call it a movie.
We called it a picture show.

The ticket cost a quarter.
A bag of popcorn cost a dime.
I would settle in
To have a fun-filled time.

The picture show began
With some silly cute cartoon.
Sometimes there was Popeye
While Olive Oyl did swoon.

When the bad guys would appear,
We knew them by their hats
For they always wore the black ones.
At these villains we hissed and spat.

The good guys then had hats
That were white with a wide brim.
As they always were the heroes,
We would encourage them.

There was usually some lady
In the hands of the bad guys.
When the good guys tried her rescue,
We'd fear for their lives.

Roy Rogers or Gene Autry
Usually wore the big white hats.
They were my movie heroes
From the place where I sat.

No cuss words were allowed
Coming from the movie screen.
There was no violence or sex.
The movies then were clean.

How I long to go back
To the Saturday picture show
Where me and my friends
On Saturdays did go.

This was a simple era
That has passed from life's scene.
Don't you wish we'd return
To movies that are clean?

3-21-04

[22] The Fence Post, Plains Edition,
August 19, 2006

Walking the Barrel

The children were bored.
What would they do?
They wanted something
All brand new.

They viewed their Dad's
Stock of things.
Fifty-gallon barrels
What fun they'd bring.

They rolled the barrels
Out in the drive.
They bet each other
They'd not survive

Walking a barrel,
Staying on top
But determined to try
And not to stop.

The brother tried balancing.
His feet didn't fit.
Then he fell
And the dust he bit.

He was determined
To try again.
He almost fell
But finally did win.

He challenged his sister
To try another
But she did better
Than her brother.

They soon were racing
Around the drive.
Feet flying fast
Who would survive?

First a slip
And then another.
Down went the sister
And then the brother.

If you want to put
Your life in peril,
Why not try
Walking a barrel?

1-21-03

[23] Nebraska Fence Post, April 5, 2003

The Party Line

Ring - ring.
It's a short and a long
To which neighbor
Does this ring belong?

Our number was
2 F 2.
To ring two shorts
Is what you'd do

If you wanted to talk
To Mother or me.
Get off the line
Was my usual plea.

For we were on
A party line.
We had no privacy
Most of the time.

My brother and his friends
Devised a plan
But those listening
Wouldn't understand.

They made up a story
About Cousin Ted
That he was hurt
And 'twas almost dead.

They called one another
On the telephone.
They could almost hear
Those listening groan,

As they spun their tale
About poor old Ted.
They said they were worried
That he was almost dead.

When they were finished,
They hung up the phone.
 It would do no harm,
If they were alone.

There were many listening,
When they spun their tale.
It was a hotter message
Than getting the mail.

Those neighbors went
To see poor old Ted
To the hospital
Before he was dead.

To their surprise
He was not there.
They had gone
To show their care.

Many calls
My Dad received

From the neighbors
My brother'd deceived.

Larry was punished
For what he'd done
But he told Dad,
"It was just in fun."

Party lines
Caused much travail.
That's the end
Of this party line tale.

8-22-02

[24] Nebraska Fence Post, December 28, 2002

The Radio

When I was a child,
We had no TV,
But we listened to the radio
Very intently.

The Lone Ranger would come on.
It held us in suspense,
As he always came
To a victim's defense.

Sky King too
Was a program we heard.
We'd listen intently
To every word.

It's Howdy Dowdy Time
Rang out o'er the air
And we'd all rush
To our radio chair.

Sergeant Preston of the Yukon
Kept law and order
Away up north
Of the Canadian border.

Fibber Magee and Molly
Would all make us laugh.
It usually came on
At the time for our bath.

Yes, there were soap operas
A way back then.
With such as "Stella Dallas"
The soap operas began.

There was the Grand Old Opera
On Saturday night
And Dad sometimes would listen
To the boxing fights.

We weren't underprivileged
`Cause we had no TV
And I think most older folks
Would agree with me.

I still like to listen
To the radio,
Even though today
To the TV I can go.

To the radio I can listen
In my home or my car,
Whether going short distances
Or traveling far.

People watching TV
Must sit and stare.
That it might become a habit
They're surely aware.

I'd love to go back
To those days long ago,

When all we had
Was the radio.

5-8-04

Walking the Fence

The corral fence
Stood six foot high.
It was made of poles
And railroad ties.

It seemed to call me,
"Come and try
To walk my fence
Before you die?"

I was then
About age eight.
I heard the challenge.
I did debate —

Could I indeed
Walk a straight line?
Would all go well?
Would I do fine?

I climbed three poles
To reach the top.
I did not pause!
I did not stop!

I put my feet
On a railroad tie.
To stand up
I then did try.

My, it's high!
If I fall down,
I know it'll hurt,
When I hit the ground.

Slowly I stood
And balanced there.
Of this height
I was aware.

I took one step
And almost fell
But on this danger
I did not dwell.

On wobbly legs
I walked that pole.
To conquer it
Had been my goal.

I had done it!
A Victor was I!
I had conquered it
One couldn't deny.

Because I'd succeeded
And walked the pole,
I knew I could accomplish
Most any goal.

All fears in life
I would quench,

When I'd remember
Walking that fence.

11-28-02

Watermelon Thief

In Dad's field
Just south of our home
Was a watermelon patch
Which no one could roam.

"To the watermelon patch
Don't go," Mom said,
But I took with me
My wagon which was red.

I also took
My best pal.
`Twas not a boy.
`Twas not a gal.

It was a dog
Whose name was Jim.
I knew that I
Could depend on him

To help me find
The sweetest melon.
Is a watermelon thief
Really a felon?

The watermelon patch
Was planted by Dad.
If I found a ripe melon,
I'd make Mom glad.

That I had gone
And disobeyed.
Around that patch
Many watermelons laid.

I thumped with my fingers
The first melon I saw
But old Jim Dog
Was scratching with his paw

On a watermelon
That was big in size.
He sniffed with his nose.
I thought he's wise.

So, I picked that melon,
Placed it in the bed
Of my little old wagon.
Back to home I sped.

When Mom saw my melon,
She started to scold.
"We'll see if it's ripe,"
Is what I was told.

She stuck the knife in
And it split clean apart.
She then tasted
A bite of the heart.

"Louise, how'd you do it?
You picked a ripe melon."

How Jim Dog found it
I began tellin'.

I was so glad
That I hadn't caused grief.
And no longer felt
I was a watermelon thief.

6-16-03

[25] Nebraska Fence Post, October 25, 2003

Chapter 3
Chores

Beans for Supper

Long ago
And far away
Mom would cook beans
On a cold winter day.

It usually was served
With hot cornbread
And that is how
We kids were fed.

That beans were for supper
We became aware,
When we'd come in
From the cold winter air.

Sometimes they were great northern
And sometimes pinto beans.
That's what we ate,
When times were lean.

In the summer we ate potato salad
Baked beans and fried chicken.
These combinations
Were certainly finger lickin'.

Kids today
Seldom eat cooked beans
For times are better
And no longer lean.

Still in this modern day
I keep a big sack
Of dry pinto beans
In my pantry out back.

I still enjoy
A pot of cooked beans.
It is a part
Of my cooking scene.

I'm not from
Society that's upper
For I'm still one
Who enjoys beans for supper.

7-31-05

Cob-Picking Days

My brother and I
Had to go
Out to the pigpen
When temperatures were low.

Our job was to gather
The empty corncobs.
We didn't like it
But it was our jobs.

The cobs would be used
To kindle a fire
In the cast iron stove
Which was Mom's desire.

I remember one day,
When the temperature was low
And the ground was frozen
Wherever we'd go.

I'd gathered about
A dozen cobs,
When I thought of a plan
To get out of that job.

If I could only
Provoke my brother
To hitting me
Then I'd run tell Mother.

I nagged at him
`Till he got real mad.
He threw at me
The frozen cobs he had.

He hit me squarely
On the head.
It broke the skin
And how it bled.

I went to Mother
And told her my plight.
"Your brother will gather
The cobs tonight,"

She said to me.
I felt delight
But I knew I was guilty
For causing the fight.

When my brother came in,
Mother really praised him
For the basket he brought
Was filled to the brim.

She fixed him a cup
Of something hot to drink
And it caused me to stop
And think — think — think.

Even a child
Is known by his ways.

If you shirk your job,
You'll get no praise.

8-20-02

[26] Nebraska Fence Post, November 30, 2002

Bottle of Tonic

When I was little,
I was sickly and thin.
No beauty pageant
Would I ever win.

So what was the solution
In those long ago days?
A nasty tasting tonic
Was to have curing ways.

Tonic was the choice
Of medicine you see.
This was the solution
Mother used on me.

I was thin and little
With a small appetite.
What I ate then
Were small, small bites.

Out would come the bottle
Of tonic each day.
`Cause of the small appetite
I had to pay

By taking two tablespoons
Before each meal.
I thought up a solution
For this awful ordeal.

I'd pile the food
Upon my plate.
To keep from taking tonic
I ate and ate.

The tonic I took
Had a terrible taste.
It cost too much
For me to waste.

I remember one day
How I was laughed at.
I dumped out the tonic
And my brother did rat.

"You're such a baby.
Just wait and see.
I'll take the tonic
And it won't affect me."

He swallowed the medicine
And he turned green.
What immediately followed
Was an awful scene.

He ran to the bathroom
And vomit he did.
My delight and laughter
I never once hid.

I ate and ate
And was still thin

But the battle over tonic
I finally did win.

In the end my thinness
Was not chronic
But it wasn't because
Of a bottle of tonic.

12-13-04

Milking Memories

I began milking cows
That were alive
When I was about
The age of five.

I would take two teats,
One in each hand
And milk and milk
To beat the band.

At first all I did
Was pull and pull
 But that cow's bag
Remained quite full.

I soon learned the trick
Of squeezing the teat.
For the art of milking
I was quite fit.

On a one legged stool,
Pail between my knees,
Those cows I'd milk.
My parents to please.

I became an expert
At squirting milk streams
At the waiting cats
Then their faces they'd clean.

To catch the milk
They'd jump in the air.
Next I'd squirt my brother
Somewhere on the hair.

If Dad didn't see,
A war would begin.
`Twas a battle I'd lose
For I'd never win.

Milk in the hair
Was but a small thing,
When to the milk house,
My bucket I'd bring.

It now was full
Of the rich, white gold.
You've done quite well,
I was told.

I'd hurry back
To milk another cow,
But there was a problem.
I'll now tell you how.

This next cow was grumpy
And didn't like me.
She didn't want to be milked
It was plain to see.

She kept kicking the bucket
From between my knees.

It made me angry
For she was hard to please.

She next switched her tail
Across my face.
Oh, how it stung
So I slackened my pace.

My bucket was finally
Almost half full,
When she stepped in it,
It took its toll.

With anger I got up
And found the kickers.
I hobbled her
For now I'd licked her

I tied her tail
To the kicker's chain.
Into a clean bucket
I milked what remained.

When I had finished,
I let her go.
She was a hard one to milk,
I want you to know.

Now that I'm grown
And live in town,
There aren't any cows
Just hanging around.

Still at night
Cows are in my dreams.
I'm squirting milk
At all sorts of things.

When that grouchy old cow
Gets her foot stuck,
It's at this point
That I wake up.

Milking for me
Is a thing of the past
But it's a memory of mine
That will always last.

1-4-02

[27] Nebraska Fence Post, July 20, 2002

The Butter Churn

Mother poured cream
Into the gallon churn.
After replacing the lid
I began to turn.

I turned and turned
The wooden handle
Which was connected
To two wooden paddles.

I turned and turned
`Till I thought I'd drop
But I knew better
Than to try to stop.

My arm was so tired
That I wanted to cry
But if I slowed down,
My Mom would ask why.

Had I reached my goal?
Could I see the cream?
Had it changed colors
Or was Mom being mean?

Just when I thought
I was about to drop,
I couldn't turn the handle
And I had to stop.

Within the churn
The cream turned to butter.
"It took long enough,"
Is what I did mutter.

Mother took the lid off.
The butter was now gold.
She worked in some salt.
"Just to taste it," I'm told.

The taste of the butter
Was quite a delight
But that old churn
I wanted out of my sight.

Saturdays came
And my Saturdays were spent
By churning the butter.
That's how Saturdays went.

I'd like to go back
To those simpler days
Where churning the butter
Meant simpler ways.

For a taste of fresh butter
I often do yearn
And I'd gladly crank
That old butter churn.

8-3-01

[2S] Nebraska Fence Post, March 9, 2002

The Barn

Withered and no paint
With sagging doors,
You must walk with care
Across her floors.

The haymow is empty
Where once it held hay
Where the children came
To romp and play.

Once within her walls
Many sounds were heard.
The thought of being quiet
Was quite absurd.

There were pigs that grunted
And roosters that crowed.
The barn was then
A safe abode.

As I stand in the door,
 I remember the past.
I had thought those times
Would always last.

I remember the days
I'd snuggle in the hay
And would play with the kittens
That were there that day.

I remember the streams
Of rich, white gold
That streamed into the bucket
That each did hold.

Within that barn
With milk we did fight,
Whenever Dad
Was out of sight.

I would squirt milk
In my brother's hair.
He'd *return* the squirt.
He didn't care where.

When Dad would return,
We were doing our chore.
Could Dad ask
For anything more?

A rope from the rafters
And we made a swing.
We'd pretend we were Tarzan
And that sort of thing.

When company came,
All us kids would go
Out to the barn
Where no grown-up would know

What we were doing
Or the stories we'd tell.

I remember one time
When our neighbor boy fell,

Out of the loft
And broke his arm.
What fear it caused
And what alarm.

The barn is now silent
And stands alone.
When I think of it,
I think of home.

11-29-01

[29] Nebraska Fence Post, January 25, 2003

The Obstinate Hen

When I was a child
Out on the farm,
There wasn't much
That would cause me harm.

I had the task
Of gathering eggs.
Sometimes I'd do it
On wobbly legs.

For there was a hen
That wanted to stay
On her eggs
That she did lay.

She was grouchy,
When I came near.
She'd puff up her feathers
Which caused me fear.

For she had a sharp beak
And would try to bite,
When I tried to shoo her
Out of my sight.

She'd stand her ground
In the box filled with hay.
She always refused
To be chased away.

I was determined
To gather her egg.
I'd heard her cackle,
When one she laid.

I went and got
Dad's thick leather glove.
I put it on
And then I shoved

That grouchy old hen
Off of her nest.
I gathered her egg.
I had done my best

When I told Mom
About my day,
She told me
To let her stay

On her nest.
Just let her be.
She'll no longer
Peck you see

Even today
It seems a sin
I had to let
That mean hen win.

8-10-02

[30] Nebraska Fence Post, November 1, 2003

My Grandfather Clock

My grandfather clock
Stood stately and tall.
It demanded respect
From its place on the wall.

Its voice was quite deep
And spoke with such power,
As it faithfully stood
And rang out the hour.

It watched us come home
At five or at two
But kept to itself
The things we would do.

As its pendulum swung
With a regular beat,
It seemed to keep time
To the marching of feet.

Some feet were quite big
And some feet were quite small
But all marched before
The clock on the wall.

It seems to see
Whenever we're down.
It also sees,
When we smile or we frown.

It makes no reply
`Bout the things it sees.
It makes no requests,
As the time quickly flees.

I've learned from the clock
To be steady and true
And to keep on doing
The things that I do.

My clock never quits
Or runs off to play.
It never complains
But keeps ticking away.

My grandfather clock,
Standing stately and tall,
Has taught me much
From its place on the wall.

Tick — tick — tock!
Tick — tick — tock!
I really admire
My grandfather clock.

8-10-01

Ironing Days

When I was a child
About the age of six,
I'd gather my ironing
Which was a mix

Of handkerchief, scarves
And white tea towels.
I'd help my mother
For we were pals.

I'd sprinkle my ironing
Just like I saw Mother
And roll them up,
One after another.

My ironing board
Was made of wood.
It was two feet high,
When by it I stood.

I'd set my ironing board
Up in the room
And then I would iron
While humming a tune.

I used a flatiron
About three inches long.
It was all mine
For to me it belonged.

I'd check to see,
If my iron was hot,
For I didn't want
To scorch a spot

On the tea towel
I was ironing just then.
Back and forth
Across the fabric I'd send.

I felt so proud
That I could help Mother.
I'd iron one piece
And then another.

I would grow tired,
As I ironed away,
For the work must be done
For it is ironing day.

In our modem culture
Not much ironing is done.
I remember a time,
When for me it was fun

To see the stack
Of fresh ironed things
I had done on my board.
What memories it brings.

My memories of ironing
Will always last

Though ironing days
Are most a thing of the past.

Ironing days.

2-21-02

Wash Day Memories

Wash day was always
A big affair.
Of this fact as a child
I was aware.

Right after breakfast
The work began.
It was work for women
And not for man.

The old wringer washer
We would roll
To its place on the porch
Where for hours we'd toil
.

Around the washer
Benches would be moved,
Though the boards on the porch
Were deeply grooved.

Next we'd fill the tub
Of the washing machine
With the hottest water
That we could bring.

The tub for the bleach water
We next would fill.
The two other tubs
Would fulfill the bill

For the washing day
To now begin.
`Twas the work for women
And not for men.

In the tub of cold water
The clothes were soaked
Then through the wringer
They carefully were poked.

When the dasher, soap and water
Had done their thing,
By a stick from the washer
The clothes we'd bring.

Run them through the wringer
Into the bleach water.
Then into the next tub
Mother taught daughter.

One had to be careful
Your fingers didn't catch.
If you did in the wringer
There was a safety latch.

Finally the clothes went
Through the wringer once more
And into a basket
That was placed on the floor.

Wash day back then
Had no perks.

For those that did it
It was simply hard work.

These memories of wash day
Are from the past
But for me
They'll always last.

Wash day memories!

7-12-03

[31] Nebraska Fence Post, August 7, 2004

Winter Dryer

Have you ever seen
Clothes stiff as a board
And it wasn't because
Starch into them was poured.

This is what happened
When temperatures were low,
If you took the wash
And to the clothesline did go.

With ting-a-ling fingers
You hung up the clothes
And soon they'd be stiff.
Yes, soon they were froze.

Sometime later
We'd take the clothes down.
`Twas the same in the country,
As it was in town.

We'd take the clothes in
And place them near the heater.
They reminded me of
Some ghostly creature.

They'd lose their stiffness,
As they became warm.
As they'd return
To their original form.

That's what we did
In days that were prior
To the invention
Of modern-day dryers.

My memory of cold fingers
And frozen clothes will last
But that's how we dried clothes
In the days that are past.

11-2-03

[32] Nebraska Fence Post, January 17, 2004

The Intruder

One warm summer morning
To the outhouse I did go.
The two-seater wasn't very tall.
It really was quite low.

I settled in for a spell
To plan my day ahead.
To do my business in a hurry
I really was not led.

I took the catalogue
That was by me on the seat
And looked at pictures in it
Of things I thought were neat.

I don't know what brought my attention
To what was coming in the door
But it was a great big snake
Headed for me across the floor.

I began to scream and holler
`Cause I thought that I would die.
My eyes were blinded by my tears,
As I began to cry.

I jumped up on the seat
Where I had sat before
But that old snake —
Kept coming across the floor.

I tried to climb the walls
But no handhold could I get.
I knew I was a goner.
My fate I now had met.

I prayed Mom would hear me
Before it was too late.
I really needed someone's help.
For it I could not wait

That snake lifted up his head.
 He was almost at my feet,
When Mom arrived with her rake,
My rescue to complete.

She carried that old snake
Out to the northern trees
And I exited that outhouse
Upon my wobbly knees.

Whenever to it I'd return,
I always shut the door.
I never wanted again to see
A snake come across the floor.

11-25-01

[33] Nebraska Fence Post, August 17, 2002

Saturday Night Baths

Back in the forties,
Whether we liked it or not,
A Saturday night bath
Is what we got.

The water was carried and
On the stove it was heated,
Then poured in a tub
Which was always greeted

By arguing and struggles
About who would be first.
The last one to bathe
Always felt cursed.

On the kitchen floor
A washtub was placed.
To be quickly bathed
Each child raced,

`Specially in the winter
For the room was cold.
"Quickly bathe,"
Is what we were told.

The water was hot,
When you first got in.
The same water was used
Again and again.

We didn't linger
Or soak for a while.
As a child,
This was never our style.

We always washed
Each night in the sink
But a complete bath we took
Just once a week.

Children today
Would have no respect
For a once-a-week bath.
They sure would object.

My children today
Always laugh,
When I tell of the experience
Of a Saturday night bath.

11-13-03

[34] The Fence Post, Plains Edition, October 21, 2006

The Kerosene Lamp

Have you ever read
By a kerosene light,
When it is dark?
When it is night?

When I was a child,
It was this way.
By a kerosene light
We also did play.

Cards, checkers, and dominoes
Was each a game
That we played,
When neighbors came.

The light from the lamp
Was then dim
But we were all
Happy within.

I still can smell
The lamp's burning wick
The odor of it
Never made me sick.

When you lit the lamp
And turned the wick too high,
It would smoke up the glass chimney
And make you cry.

It was a fine job
To trim it just so.
When lit, the light
Throughout the room would go.

We'd all gather around
The light you see:
Mom, Dad and all
We children three.

The light from the lamp
Made a warm glow
That can't be achieved
From today's light that we know.

When the lights go out
On a stormy night,
A kerosene lamp
Is still the source of my light.

1-5-04

The Treadle Sewing Machine

Whir! Whir! Whir!
I was doing my own thing.
Up and down I treadled
On that treadle sewing machine.

When learning then to sew,
I'd start it with my hand
On the wheel above
Then treadle to beat the band.

The seams would be smooth,
If I kept a steady pace.
Up and down! Up and down!
I wasn't in a race.

There was no electric motor.
My feet produced the power,
As I sat at that machine
Hour after hour.

Sometimes I'd break a needle
So I'd have to lift the arm
And I would replace it,
No cause for an alarm.

There was a round bobbin
That often needed thread
And I'd loosen the wheel
So it could wind instead.

I'd put that little bobbin
On a special made wheel.
I'd begin to treadle —
First my toe and then my heel.

How fast I did treadle,
As the bobbin went 'round and 'round.
Then suddenly I'd stop
For the bobbin had been wound.

I'd replace the bobbin
And tighten up the wheel.
I'd add a drop of oil,
If the belt to the head did squeal.

I sewed on that machine
For at least a dozen years.
When it was given away,
I shed large salty tears.

It was a wedding present,
When it was given away.
I sew on *an* electric machine,
Whenever I sew today.

Now even in my dreams
That machine is still around
 And I am busy with my feet
Treadling up and down.

Time and time again
In my dreams I repeat the scene,

When I was learning to sew
On the treadle sewing machine.

9-1-02

The Brooder House

We shoveled white sand
On the brooder house floor.
It wasn't enough
So we shoveled some more.

We next set the brooder,
A circular thing,
And filled it with fuel
Called kerosene.

The feeders were filled
With food for the chicks.
They were made of metal
And not out of sticks.

Water was filled
In the tall glass jars.
Antiseptic was added,
Bottoms affixed to the jars.

The jars were inverted
And set on the sand.
It was quite a trick
Taking a twist of the hand.

The brooder was lit
And the room became warm.
We awaited the chicks
In bodily form.

We heard the car come.
The mail was here.
We heard the chicks peeping,
As we drew near.

We picked up the cartons
With the tiny air holes.
To raise these chicks
Became our goals.

To the brooder house
We took the chicks.
They all were yellow
And not a mix.

We took each chick,
Placed them on the sand.
They ran to the brooder
And seemed to understand

They now had a home
Where they were warm
And they would be safe,
If there was a storm.

We taught each chick
To drink and eat
And I watched them, amused
From my sandy seat.

I would sit so still
And to them I'd prove,

As they climbed o'er my lap,
That I would not move.

I'd gently reach down,
Hold their fluff to my cheek
They'd cuddle down
And did not peep.

Now when I'm quiet
Like a little mouse,
My thoughts return
To that brooder house.

1-1-02

Chapter 4
School Days

An Apple for the Teacher

In a one-room schoolhouse
Upon the plain
A "city slicker" teacher
To this schoolhouse came.

He was so wise
About city stuff
But outdoor toilets
Made a life that's rough.

He thought it a shame
That the children came
To school on horses
All across the plain.

He thought in cars
They should come to school.
Why not try
A school car pool?

He did not dress
In regular jeans
But in suits and ties
And "city slicker" things.

During Music he tried
To teach ballet
But cowboy boots
Wouldn't dance that way.

He really was shaken
By a normal thing
Like schoolhouse skunks
And the odor they bring.

The schoolhouse was full
Of smoke one day
For the "city slicker" teacher
Had tried to lay

A fire in the stove
To warm the school.
When the problem was solved,
He felt like a fool.

A student showed him
What was the answer
For he didn't know
To open the damper.

The usual tricks
Were pulled on this teacher
But a snake in his desk
Was really the grand feature.

He turned green at the gills,
He thought he was doomed
`Till the littlest child
Took the snake from the room.

As the year went by,
He lost his "city slicker" ways.

He learned from his students
The Arthur County ways.

To show he was accepted
Guess what was the feature.
It was every child brought
An apple for the teacher.

9-15-01

[35] Nebraska Fence Post, April 20, 2002

The Schoolhouse

All alone the schoolhouse stands.
Its walls are needing paint.
Weeds are growing in the yard.
It's grandeur now quite faint.

Let you and I go back in time
To days so long ago
To a one room schoolhouse by the road
Which all former students know.

Early in the morning
The teacher would arrive,
Sometimes by horse and buggy
Or whatever she could drive.

She first would build a fire
In the potbellied stove.
Its kindling usually came
From some cottonwood grove.

The children would arrive
With a lunch pail in their hand.
Their pails were then a syrup
Or an empty lard can.

They would take their seats
At the ringing of the bell,
Then rise to pledge allegiance.
They all did this quite well.

Sometimes there were students
In all eight grades.
The teacher did not have
A helper or an aide.

From the recitation bench
The subjects were on review
And the answers that were given
Were really not a few.

Reading, writing and arithmetic
Were subjects that were stressed.
When the teacher read out loud,
Is what they all liked best.

There were daily chores
The students had to do.
The dusting of the blackboards
Was one of quite a few.

Whenever a child was thirsty,
He'd raise up his hand.
Whenever given permission
By the water cooler he'd then stand

And take his tin cup
And place it beneath the spout,
Then press the silver button
`Till the water did come out.

Recess was a fun time.
All the children came,

Big and small, young and old,
Playing in whatever game.

When recess then was over
Perhaps a cipher down would soon begin.
Even the littlest child
Against an older child could win.

The littlest child would be given
A simple sum to do
While his opponent, an older child,
Would have columns of math to do.

"Turn, rise and pass"
Was how the students were dismissed.
There were always needs
For the teacher to assist

With the gathering of the coats,
Mittens and overshoes.
There was usually someone
Whose mittens they would lose.

The teacher would end her day
By sweeping up the floor.
She would heave a sigh,
As she went out the door.

The schoolhouse now is silent
It presently stands alone,
But its students will remember it
Wherever they may roam.

Little schoolhouse on the plain,
You did your job quite well.
These memories I have written
Now I bid you a fond farewell.

1-13-02

A Surefire Cure

When I was young
And went to school,
Most children thought
Chewing gum was cool.

My mom, as a teacher,
Was very wise.
She had a solution
For those gum chewing guys.

She took a jar
To the front of the room.
That she was kidding
They just assumed,

When she told them
To put their gum inside,
And by this rule
They would abide.

If you chew gum,
You must select from within
The jar of gum
That had been chewed again.

They no longer had
A smile on their face.
For someone else's gum
They had no taste.

`Cause no one wanted
To chew gum from this pool,
 It was a surefire cure
For chewing gum in school.

4-15-04

Dinner Pails

I swung the pail, as I went to school,
Its treasures then were hid.
I often dreamed, as I walked along
Of the treats beneath the lid.

Today would I have peanut butter
Or mayonnaise to eat?
Would there be a cookie
Or some candy, as a treat?

I usually found an apple
Tucked beneath its shiny brim.
My schoolmate, Bruce, might want me
To trade my lunch with him.

The pails were all lined up.
Some were lard or syrup cans,
Awaiting for the dinner bell
And eager, fresh washed hands.

With "attention, turn, rise and pass,"
We were given the okay
To march back where the pails were at
And to eat our lunch that day.

The aroma of some juicy orange
And someone's bologna meat
Are odors that teased my nose,
As we sat down to eat.

My pail was a syrup can
With a sturdy little bail

And sometimes how I struggled
With the lid on that pail.

Lunch soon would be over.
The pails were lined up in a row
And they would wait there until
Home from school we all would go.

We'd swing our pails, as we went
Across the prairie sod.
We'd say goodbye to some classmate
With the slightest farewell nod.

At last we would arrive at home
With our pails still in hand.
We'd place them in the kitchen where
Until tomorrow they would stand.

Whatever do the children do
Without a pail today?
1 think I'd rather have my pail
Than the lunches served today.

Dinner pail! Dinner pail!
Swinging from my hand.
No longer are these dinner pails
Found throughout the land.

Dinner pails!

7-31-01

[36] Nebraska Fence Post, September 1, 2001

District 55

In an Arthur County schoolhouse
Known as District 55,
It wasn't always empty
But would sometimes come alive.

Sometimes there at night
Cars would be parked outside its fence.
Adults would be inside
With the children in suspense,

For it soon would be Christmas.
There'd be a program there tonight
With all ages of the children
Suffering feelings of stage fright.

Across the front of the room
Sheets by safety pins were hung
To form the stage's curtains
Before the program had begun.

The children would take a peep
To see who all were there.
They soon would be on stage
 They were quite aware.

The teacher would begin
By welcoming all who came.
It never made a difference
That her message was the same.

Two children on each side
Would pull the curtains apart
And this was the signal
The program now would start.

Sometimes there'd be a piece
Someone had memorized.
Sometimes there'd be a play
With its actors in disguise.

There always was much singing,
Which the children did enjoy.
The audience clapped enthusiastically
For every girl and boy.

When the program finally ended,
The children all received a sack.
There were oranges, apples, nuts and candy
The teacher into these sacks had packed.

The parents were so proud
Of what their children had done.
Refreshments then were served
While the talking had begun.

When the cars all pulled away,
It was late at night.
The schoolhouse once again
Became a lonely sight.

In the hearts of former students
Treasured memories are alive

Of this Arthur County schoolhouse
Known as District 55.

4-16-04

[37] Nebraska Fence Post, December 25, 2004

The Loosened Screw

When I was about
The age of six,
The children at school
On the teacher played tricks.

There was one teacher
Who always sat
Leaning back on her chair
With her hands in her lap.

Her feet always rested
On the top of the desk
And perhaps by now
You've guessed the rest.

The boys got an idea
Of a trick to play.
They patiently waited
For just the right day.

On Monday morning,
When the teacher was late,
That it was the time
They did not debate.

The boys quickly adjusted
The screw in the chair.
That it had been loosened
We all were aware.

We all were quiet,
When the teacher arrived
In her little old car
Out in the drive.

She took off her coat
And sat in her chair.
That the screw had been loosened
We all were aware.

With bated breath
We awaited the crash,
Even though we knew
We'd get a tongue lash.

The time finally came,
When she leaned back in her chair.
We kept our eyes to the front
And at the teacher didn't stare.

Just as expected,
She flew back in a heap.
Her steady composure
She did not keep.

Her dress flew up
Away over her head.
To loosen the screw
The boys had been led.

From then on
Her feet remained on the floor.

The lesson of the screw
She couldn't ignore.

Boys will be boys
And tricks they will play
For we had to stay in
For the rest of the day.

No one told
The secret they knew
Of who was guilty
Of loosening that screw.

12-25-04

Forbidden Grapes

In District Number Eleven
The county superintendent came
And Loyal Simon
Was his name.

Soon it was recess
And the children were let out
But the older boys
Decided to prowl about.

They spied in Loyal's car
Some grapes setting there.
They talked about eating them
But would they dare?

They knew the younger children
On them would tell
And then these boys
Wouldn't be doing well.

They took the grapes
And gave some to each kid.
The guilt of these boys
Would now be hid.

The concord grapes
Left a telling stain
That they all were guilty
It was very plain.

The anger of Loyal
The boys wanted to provoke
And they hoped to get
The superintendent's "goat."

Loyal soon came out
And simply drove away.
It ruined the fun
The boys planned that day.

When my mom told this story,
One thing came into view:
If you're up to some mischief
It might turn sour on you.

2-14-05

[38] The Fence Post, Plains Edition, April 2, 2005

The Model "A"

The neighbors I knew
Had a Model "A."
They'd drive to school
Day after day.

When school was out,
We'd all pile in.
I, as the youngest,
Would wear a grin

`Cause they didn't make
Me walk from school
I wanted to ride.
I was no fool.

I was first to get off
So I wasn't inside
But on the running board
I did ride.

Oh, what fun
We all had
Until one day,
When they made me mad.

They purposely made me
Lose my hold.
I fell in a puddle
So I did scold.

"I hope you fall
In an auto gate
And you'll all end up
Being late."

The next day came.
I was no longer blue
And they let me
Ride to school.

There's never the thrill
In cars today
Like I had riding
In a Model "A."

3-01-04

Beckon! Beckon!

Beckon! Beckon!
Is what we would play
When we went out for recess
Day after day.

"Beckon, beckon, who'll give a beckon?'
The one "it" heard them cry.
We were playing a game
And the one "it" was I.

When I'd catch a person
And put him in the ring
"Beckon, beckon, I need a beckon,"
Out then he would scream.

If he saw a beckon,
Then he could go free
To hide again.
And still it I would be.

I couldn't look everywhere
For a beckon to be seen,
As hidden hands popped up,
Their beckon to bring.

If I saw a hand
And discovered where hidden,
They were caught
And had to do what was bidden.

In the prison ring
All but one were caught.
They all cried out
And a beckon each sought.

I was alert,
Looking everywhere.
"Go ahead, give a beckon.
Now do it, I dare."

Five minutes did pass
Then five minutes more.
No beckon was given,
As there'd been before.

This last person I must catch,
If I was to win.
I searched o'er the playground
Again and again.

At the edge of the playground
Was parked an old Ford.
To give a beckon
This last child ignored.

For he was caught,
As tight as can be.
Under the Ford
I now could see.

He was quite plump,
But he chose to hide there.

That he might get stuck
He wasn't aware.

The game was over,
As I pulled him out.
That eventually I'd win
I never did doubt

"Beckon, beckon, who'll give a beckon?"
Is what we did play,
When Billy got stuck
'Neath the Ford that day.

3-11-03

A Snake Challenge

When I was the youngest
Little girl in country school,
The boys all laughed at me
And said I was a fool.

I remember to this day,
When the boys all taunted me
About two bull snakes
That were so plain to see.

They said, "You're such a baby.
To touch them you're afraid."
I quickly took the challenge,
Accepting the deal they made.

They'd let me play with them,
If a "chicken" I'd not be
And would touch a snake
So all the boys could see.

Yes, with great determination
I approached those old bull snakes.
I grabbed one by the tail.
What a splash he did make,

As I flipped him in the tank
For all the boys to see.
That day there was a hero
And that hero was just me.

I didn't stop with one
But flipped the other in.
The deal that we had made
I certainly did win.

When I challenged all the boys
To come and do likewise,
They refused to do it
Which to me was a surprise.

I learned a simple lesson,
When I flipped the snakes that day,
Just face the impossible
And do not run away.

It's easy to brag and say
What all you can do
But the "proof is in the pudding"
That is done by you.

Want to flip snakes, anyone?

6-2-04

[39] The Fence Post, Plains Edition, May 14, 2005

The Recitation Bench

The recitation bench
Was about six feet long
And in modern schools
It's missing and gone.

It was there we recited
The lessons we learned.
It was there our attention
To the teacher we turned.

The bench was just down
From where I sat.
The fear of it
I'd daily combat.

When it was my turn
To go there each day,
I was tongue-tied
And didn't know what to say
.

My knees were wobbly
As I walked down the desk aisle,
But I usually was encouraged
By my teacher's smile.

When my destination was reached
And I had sat down,
I kept my eyes on the teacher
So she'd not frown.

I'd recite then my lessons
With other students or alone.
When asked a question,
I'd inwardly groan.

I was always glad
To go back to my seat,
When my time on the bench
Was then complete.

When older students came
And read from that bench,
My thirst for knowledge
They helped to quench.

Yes, the recitation bench
Found in country schools
Was one of the most
Important learning tools.

It is now gone.
It's but a memory of my mind.
Yes, the recitation bench
Was one of a kind.

6-14-05

Prince and the Buggy

An eastern teacher
Came to stay
At the Jesse Vath home
One November day.

She was pretty and trim
And oh, so polite
But I'll tell what happened
After school one night.

Each morning Ada and Helen
Drove the teacher to school.
She was a good teacher
And was no fool.

Their mode of transportation
Was a horse and buggy.
`Cause she didn't want to walk
She felt mighty lucky.

One night after school
The teacher kept some boys in.
Ada and Helen grumbled
And thought it a sin

That they couldn't go home
But they, too, had to wait.
A solution they both
Did contemplate.

Because the teacher didn't know
How to a buggy hitch a horse,
The girls would do it
Before they left, of course.

With this chore completed
The girls did walk
And how they grumbled,
As they did talk.

Over hills they walked
And were out of sight.
They'd sure beat the teacher
Home this night.

Back at the school
Prince decided not to stay
But would head for home
`Cause it was the end of the day.

With no one at the reins
He then was led
To run through a gate
That was dead ahead.

The end result
Was a torn-up buggy.
That Prince wasn't hurt
Was very lucky.

Their dad almost took
An inch off their hide

But the thing that hurt most
Was the dent in their pride.

Horses and buggies
Are a thing from the past
But this memory of Mom's
Will forever last.

2-14-05

[40]The Fence Post, Plains Edition, February 4, 2006

Buck at Bat

There was a ballgame
Played at a country school.
I was the catcher
But I was no fool.

I knew I had to stand
Away from the bat
And almost every time
I accomplished that.

With the crack of the bat
This ball game had begun.
Some boys had struck out
And some had hit a run.

The bases were loaded,
As Buck came to bat.
My eye was on the ball,
As on my heels I sat.

Strike one was the call,
As the ball kissed my glove.
For this game of baseball
I had a great love.

The next pitch was thrown.
The umpire called "ball one."
Playing baseball with the boys
For me *was* fun.

A sizzling ball came flying.
The call was "strike two."
Buck knew to hit a homer
Was the thing to do.

To me Buck seemed quite tall,
As he crouched there with his bat.
I simply pulled down tighter
My red hat.

I watched the ball coming,
As Buck swung with all his might
But what resulted was
My day turning into night.

With that mighty swing
Buck had struck me on the head.
As I crumpled to the ground,
The boys thought that I was dead.

I lay there quite still
But soon I came around.
I simply picked myself up
From my place upon the ground.

I had a lump on my head
That was very fat
But I was more careful
Whenever Buck was at the bat.

3-8-06

[41] The Fence Post, Plains Edition, April 22, 2006

Chapter 5
Pets

Pete, the Star

Long ago
On the Jesse Vath Farm
A runt was saved
From suffering harm.

He was the last piglet
That night to be born.
He was little in size
Yet perfect in form.

There weren't enough teats
To go around
So no milk for him
Could be found.

Jesse rescued that piglet,
His life to save,
And unto Daughter Helen
This piglet he gave.

A pop bottle was filled
With warm milk from a cow.
A rubber nipple was added.
Now the piglet had "chow."

Helen gave him the name
Of Pete one day
And with Helen
This piglet did play.

Wherever Helen went
Pete could be found.
Soon he was eating ground corn
From his trough on the ground.

When Pete was full grown
And to market he must go,
He was taken
To the Denver Stock Show.

After Pete was scrubbed up
And stood with the rest,
In Helen's eyes
He was the best.

From being a runt pig
Pete had come far
But who would have guessed
He'd be a stock show star?

We never know
Who'll become famous and big
Even if you are
An Arthur County pig.

2-2-05

[42] The Fence Post, Plains Edition, September 10, 2005

Old Bill

When I was a child,
We had a horse named Bill.
Though fifty years have passed
I remember him still.

He was a horse
That was gentle as can be.
Sometimes there were six,
Including me

That would climb on his back
To go for a ride.
That he loved children
He did not hide.

When on purpose
We'd slide off his tail,
To stop at once
Bill never did fail.

A blizzard came
In "forty-nine"
And a sad sight
My father did find.

Gentle old Bill
Had slipped on the ice.
A broken leg
Was old Bill's price.

Dad had to put him
Out of his misery
Though Dad knew how much
He was loved by me.

Though he was a horse
He had a purpose to fulfill.
To appreciate life
Was taught me by old Bill.

10-18-05

[43] The Fence Post, Plains Edition, March 18, 2006

A Grandma's Dilemma

I'd like to tell a truth
And which isn't a yarn
About an incident that occurred
On the Jesse Vath farm.

There were two young girls
Who had many pets.
About one of these
They have memories yet.

A thin little grandma
Also lived on this farm.
She was afraid of things
That might do her harm.

There was an outhouse
To which she would go.
What she'd do in it
We all do know.

There was a little problem
She daily did face.
The girls' pet ram
To this outhouse would race.

Around and around
This outhouse he would go.
When Grandma was in it
He seemed always to know.

She'd scream and holler
For the girls to come.
All that was needed
Was only one

To come and lead
The pet ram away
And she'd be safe
For another day.

Sometimes the girls
Pretended not to hear
And this caused the grandma
Anxiety and fear.

Sometimes they were tempted
To let the ram go.
What would happen to Grandma
They wanted to know,

But they were good girls
And made right decisions,
As they daily went
On these rescue missions.

Memories of these dilemmas
Will always last
Though outhouses are now
A thing of the past.

7-2-04

Sam, the Ram

We had a pet sheep
That was a ram.
We'll just call him
By the name of Sam.

When he was a lamb
And could hardly toddle,
I fed Sam
From a baby bottle.

Even as a lamb
He had a strong mind.
After he grew up
I'll tell of a time

That he was mischievous
And loved to bunt.
He'd attack from the back
But never from the front.

We had two bachelors
That visiting came.
The Freeman Brothers
Were their names.

One was tall and thin.
The other was short and stout.
They got out of their pickup
And turned about.

I watched them walk
Toward me in the drive.
I wondered what'll happen
If Sam does arrive.

Sam doesn't always listen
To an authoritative call,
Especially from me,
A girl who was small.

What I saw next
From the corner of my eyes
Was Sam's head bent low
And heading for those guys.

The brothers looked up
With fear on each face
And with great speed
To their pickup they raced.

With his long legs flying
Walt reached safety first
But Bud with short legs
Needed an energy boost

Which he got
From Sam's lowered head,
As he bunted him into
The pickup bed.

After this happened
Dad knew what to do.

Sam's bunting days
Were soon to be through.

Dad loaded him up.
Sam was docile and meek.
Sam, the ram, was sold
That very same week.

This was a true happening
And is not a yarn
But is a long ago incident
On the Williams' farm.

6-30-04

[44] The Fence Post, Plains Edition, January 22, 2005

Goosey, Goosey, Gander

Fifty-six years
Have now gone by
But I remember a goosey gander
That made me cry.

I loved to go
Outdoors and play
But there was a gander
That held me at bay.

Daily I tried
To sneak out of the yard
But every single time
He was on his guard.

He'd rush at me
And hiss and hiss
But he wasn't saying,
"I'll give you a kiss."

Instead he was trying
To take a bite you see
Out of my legs,
As I did flee.

Many a day
Me he did bite.
To my brother
It was a funny sight

Then one day
I got smart
And turned over
His applecart.

You see, I now
Had a board in my hand
And I became
The one in command.

I chased that gander
And he did flee.
Now the gander
Was afraid of me.

Goosey gander is,
As goosey gander does
But for this goosey gander
I never had love.

8-16-04

[45] The Fence Post, Plains Edition, July 7, 2007

Babe

Babe was just a calf
Who would grow into a cow.
We didn't understand
Why her mother would allow

My brother, Jerry, to lead her
Around our little corral,
Or why Babe's mother did not bunt
Jerry, if he fell.

As Spring turned to Summer
And Babe began to grow,
She would follow Jerry
Wherever he would go.

When she became a yearling
And before she would turn two,
Jerry thought he'd ride her.
It seemed the thing to do.

As Jerry climbed upon her back
And then settled for a ride.
He soon was riding her around.
She was his greatest pride.

Every evening around four
He'd climb upon Babe's back
To go out to the hills and
Then he'd give her slack,

He would speak a word to her
To turn left or right
And they would bring the cows in
To be milked again that night.

Babe really had a problem.
She thought she was a horse — not a cow
But ride Babe to school
Dad would not allow,

Babe! Babe! Babe!
You're a memory from our past.
It's only a childhood memory
But a memory that'll last.

8-1-01

[46]Nebraska Fence Post, November 10, 2001

Bambi

Bambi was
A baby deer.
How he became my pet
Is really not clear.

One day he arrived
At the kitchen door.
He was shaking
And kind of poor.

I put my arms
Around this deer.
I tried to calm
All of his fear.

He needed milk
So I filled a bottle,
While on his legs
He continued to waddle.

He began to calm down,
As I stroked his back.
Could I provide
The things that he lacked?

A teat was added
To the bottle.
I gave it to him
And the milk he did swallow.

His first night with me
I slept on the floor.
His slightest whimper
I did not ignore.

He lay so still
Beside me on the rug.
All night long
His neck I did hug.

I fed him again
When morning came.
Again at noon
I did the same.

Weeks went by
And he did grow.
When he wanted to play,
He told me so.

When I hung clothes
Upon the line,
He butted me
But he did not whine.

`Twas his way of saying,
"Come play with me."
He didn't understand
It was plain to see.

Later that Spring
Someone opened the door

And with three bounds
He came across the floor.

He'd then place his neck
`Cross the back of mine.
He'd do this
Almost every time.

One morning I arose
And called him to come
But there was no response
From my little one.

I found him all bloody
And dead on the lawn.
I began crying
"What happened to my fawn?"

It seemed the dogs
Had killed him that day
For they were too rough,
When they wanted to play.

I dug a grave
By the bushes for him
And when he was buried,
I sang a hymn.

That day dragged by
And then it was tomorrow.
I still didn't know how
To express my sorrow.

We had a black dog
By the name of Jim.
I poured out my sorrow
Unto him.

Little by little
The sorrow passed.
Other pets I accepted
At last.

There were other pets
That belonged to me
But never another
Like my little Bambi.

2-24-02

Sugar, the Shetland Pony

Out of the house
The grandkids were sent.
So to the calf pasture
They all went.

There were four grandkids,
Two girls and two boys.
They were too old
For regular toys.

There was one thing
That they could do.
They could ride the Shetland
The whole day through.

After bridling the Shetland
And bringing him in
It was time
For the fun to begin.

Little did they know
Sugar had a plan.
He didn't want to be rode
By pint-sized man.

First one kid would get on
And go for a ride.
This intolerance for children
Sugar didn't hide.

He'd run real fast
But would stop on a dime.
He got rid of his rider
Almost every time.

When the next kid got on
To go for a ride,
To rub the rider off
He then would decide.

Sugar had a habit
That caused some fright.
It was by taking
Out of them a bite.

Sometimes there was a problem
`Cause he would get out of control.
To have his own way
Was always his goal.

After riding this pony
Long and quite fast,
Grandpa came saying,
"Kids, this ride is the last."

This Shetland seemed to say
To these children of men,
"Ha! Ha! In the end
I did win."

6-11-05

[47] The Fence Post, Plains Edition, May 27, 2006

Buttons

Buttons was but
A coal-black pup.
Though from a large litter
She couldn't suck.

She was born beneath
The milk house floor.
Her constant whimpering
I couldn't ignore.

To the house I carried her
To get her warm.
She was a runt,
Small in form.

With an eyedropper
Warm milk I fed her.
She was so thin
Bones showed through her fur.

I wrapped her in a towel
To keep her warm.
A box by the stove
She didn't scorn.

I carefully fed her
Every hour or two.
Mom said if she lives,
It's up to you.

All through the night
A vigil I'd keep.
I watched this puppy
With almost no sleep.

With my loving care
She rallied around
And she began crawling
When placed on the ground.

Soon she was lapping
Milk from a bowl.
To make her live
Had been my goal.

She lived and became
A lively pet
But her story is not
Finished yet.

We had too many dogs
So I gave her away
But in the city
She would not stay.

She always wanted
To come back home
So she took to wandering
And the streets she did roam.

She met her demise
Neath the wheels of a truck.

I heard from her owners
Of Buttons' bad luck.

Buttons! Buttons!
You were my friend.
I guess that is how
Her story must end.

Buttons!

12-31-01

Chapter 6
Hard Work

Spring Plowing

Spring, as a child,
Was the time for birth
And also the time
For the plowing of earth.

To the field each day
My dad would go.
Straight furrows in it
He'd make, you know.

As he'd turn the earth,
The dirt felt damp and cool.
To do this job
A plow was his tool.

At the edge of such field
I would go and sit down,
Take off my shoes
And play around

In the deep plowed furrow
With dirt between my toes.
The thrill of it
The country child knows.

The fresh smell of the earth
Is called ozone today
That came up from the furrows
Where as a child I would play.

Most farmers go no longer
And plow the fields.
They've new methods of farming
To get better crop yields.

I'll always remember
The plowed furrow rows
And its cool, damp earth
Where I wiggled my toes.

Though times have changed
And the farmers have new ways,
I'll always remember
Past spring plowing days.

4-11-05

[48] Nebraska Rodeo Review, 2006

The Stacking of the Hay

In July we'd begin stacking
The wild prairie hay
And this we would do
Day after day.

Early to the fields
Our family would go.
Dad would rake the hay
And Mom and boys would mow.

After letting it cure
In the hot summer sun
The stacking of hay
Was really not fun.

A sweeper was used
To gather the hay
And take it to the stacker
Throughout the hot day.

An overshot stacker
Our family did use.
To get up on the stack
I adamantly refused.

Horses pulled the cable
Which lifted up the stacker teeth.
Sometimes the load of hay
Would cover the man beneath

Who was standing on the haystack
Packing down the hay.
Me get on the stack?
No way! No way! No way!

Today times have changed
And modern equipment is used.
To get on the haystack
I need no longer refuse.

`Cause that's now how modern man
Stacks the prairie hay.
I'll always remember stacking
The old-fashioned way.

6-24-05

[49] The Fence Post, Plains Edition, July 23, 2005

Dad's Water Jug

Long ago when
Men worked in the fields,
They gathered the grain
That the fields did yield.

What did they do
When they were hot and dry?
What exactly for a drink
Did they try?

My dad had a solution
To meet this need,
Whether gathering the harvest
Or planting the seed.

He'd take a gallon jug
Where vinegar had previously been
And wash it out
`Till it was clean within.

He then would take burlap,
Wrap it firm and tight
Around this jug.
It was a strange sight.

Early in the morning
Water was placed within.
The outside burlap
Would be soaked again.

To the fields this water jug
Would be taken this way
For the men to drink from
Throughout the day.

The wet burlap
Kept the water cool.
I'd not have thought of it.
So, what would you do?

I always wanted
To give Dad a hug,
When I would drink
From Dad's water jug.

5-10-04

[50] Nebraska Fence Post, September 25, 2004

The Threshing Machine

There she stood
Dressed in gray,
The threshing machine
Where I loved to play.

After harvest she was parked
In the eastern trees.
She had a fascination,
Especially for me.

I remember the first time
I opened her side door
 And her inner bowels
I began to explore.

I followed her cavity
Up rows of slats and teeth
`til I emerged at her top
From her bowels beneath.

The door on top
Allowed me to crawl
Out of her belly
Because I was small.

Once on top
I felt like a king,
As I began dreaming
Of wars and such things.

The blower could be moved
Out from its side
And many times on it
We kids did ride.

A wheel you could turn
Hand over hand
Until the blower was extended,
As far as we planned.

From this metal machine
Imaginary wars were fought
Until Mother called
Then the wars were forgot

I'd have one in my yard,
If today I could choose
But threshing machines
Are no longer used.

Now it sits in a graveyard
Of out dated machines
But I remember the fun
That once it did bring.

When I see one there
Still dressed in gray,
I remember the threshing machine fun
Of that long-ago day.

5-20-06

[51] Nebraska Fence Post, August 23, 2003

Threshing Days

The neighbors came
From far and wide.
Their hard work ethic
They did not hide.

Some came in pickups
And others by car.
Some traveled ten miles
Which then seemed far

To help with the harvest.
It was threshing day.
They all came freely
And expected no pay.

The threshing machine
Was pulled to the field.
Would the grain that's threshed
Be of high or low yield?

The threshing machine's belt
Caused the farmer to fret
If this belt to the tractor
Wasn't properly set.

Some men and strong boys
Rode hayracks to the field.
After pitching the shocks on
Their shirts they peeled

For it was hard work
And the sun was hot
But these hard workers
Would not stop

`Till the hayrack was full
And on its way.
They could always rest
At the end of the day.

The threshing machine
Growled like a bear,
As it awaited the shocks
That would be pitched through the air.

The hayrack arrived
At the threshing machine.
The bundles were pitched in
`Till the hayrack was clean.

The machine began belching
Out straw from one end
And out to one side
The clean grain it did send.

The men all worked
`Till it was high noon,
As they went to the house,
They knew they'd eat soon

Platters of meat
And vegetables galore,

Hot biscuits just baked
And still there was more

Puddings and cakes
And fresh-baked pies
Were not to these men
Even a little surprise.

As the men had been working,
The women had been too
For they were preparing
The food for this crew.

As they talked 'round the table,
It didn't really matter
If more than one talked.
There was a constant chatter.

Dinner soon was over
And the men rose to go.
'Twas a mighty fine dinner, Ma'am,
I want you to know."

The men worked hard
Throughout the day
But when they went home,
They wanted no pay.

Neighbors helped neighbors
In days gone past.
This is a memory
That will always last.

I'll look to help others
In different ways,
As I always remember,
Those threshing days.

9-28-01

No Chicken for Dinner

When I was but
A wee little thing,
My dad ran
A threshing machine.

With a tractor he'd pull it
O'er hills to each farm.
The noise it made
Was a certain alarm

To the farmer's wife
There'd be men for dinner.
She thought I'll fix chicken.
It'll sure be a winner.

She'd run outside
And select a chicken.
It was sure to be
Quite "finger lickin'."

Dad's threshing crew
Always knew their fate.
What they'd have for dinner
Was never a debate.

Chicken was for lunch
And chicken was for dinner.
It always seemed
That chicken was the winner.

Can you imagine eating
Nothing but chicken
And it was not always
"Finger lickin'."

You can't blame the cook
For it was fresh meat.
There was no market
Just down the street.

Sometimes it was cooked done
And sometimes it was not.
Sometimes with noodles
It was cooked in a pot.

When the threshing was complete
And Dad would come home,
He always made
His wishes known.

What we'd have for dinner
Was never to be chicken,
No matter how tasty
Or how "finger lickin'."

Now that I'm older
I do understand
Why chicken for dinner
Was seldom our plan.

With refrigeration today
We have a good deal

And don't need to have
Chicken *every* meal.

For Dad's threshing crew
Chicken was always the winner
But I still hear Dad say,
"Please, no chicken for dinner."

11-2-03

[52] The Fence Post, Plains Edition, November 4, 2006

Branding Time

When the cattle would be gathered
In corrals out by the barn,
Branding time had come
To us on the farm.

Neighbors would arrive.
Some would bring their horses too.
No one had to tell
These men what to do.

The calves born late in winter
Would all have need of brands.
Being separated from their mothers
These calves did not understand.

Part of this crew were boys.
They'd choose the calf that's next.
They'd throw the calf and stretch him
And they never were perplexed

About how to hold them,
Placing each hoof next to their chest.
The branding iron was then applied
But these boys didn't get a rest.

Castrating and dehorning
Were two more things to do
That were done at branding time
Before the calves were through.

When I was just a young girl,
Girls didn't help with branding time
But ranchers now use girls.
They get along just fine.

Whenever spring arrives
Smells of brandings are all there.
Blood, manure and cattle
And singed hair are in the air.

I now live in a town
And I usually do quite fine
But I still have a longing
To go home at branding time.

3-22-04

Corn Picking

Off to the field
With the team we'd go.
We hoped to be done
Before the arrival of snow.

A big cornfield
Before us lay.
We'd do what we could
Before the close of day.

With gloves on both hands
And a corn hook over one
The fall picking of the corn
Had now begun.

We'd line the horses up
To go straight down the row.
When coming to the end
They always seemed to know.

They'd start out slow
With one hoof before another.
The family would follow
Except for little brother.

He'd always ride
In the corn wagon.
"I'll pick more than you,"
My brother began braggin'.

That's all it took
To challenge me.
I was determined to pick
The most you see.

With a swipe of the corn hook
The husks were removed
And a flick of the wrist
My worth was proved.

The clean ears of corn
Were then thrown into the wagon.
I soon made my brother
Stop his pesky braggin'.

Dad picked two rows
While Mom picked one.
We kids thought the picking
Was really great fun.

We all would walk
Beside the corn wagon.
Larry's and my efforts
Weren't really worth the braggin'.

It took several weeks
To pick a cornfield
And we were sure proud
Of each field's yield.

What took us weeks
Today takes but a few hours

For now they have combines
With corn picking power.

Gone are the horses
And now gone is the wagon
But for those bygone days
I'm continually thankin'.

These are my memories
Of corn picking that I've penned
And now it's the time
For this poem to end — THE END.

8-24-05

[53] The Fence Post, Plains Edition, November 5, 2005

Feeding the Crew

I remember Mother
Would have to make
One more pie
Or one more cake.

You see tomorrow
There'd be a branding crew.
She knew the things
That she must do.

She knew that early
She must rise,
If she was to feed
All of those guys.

Platters of fried chicken
And a huge, huge roast
Was some of the meat
That I liked the most,

When Mother spread a meal
For the crew to eat,
When they'd come in
And take a seat.

There were real mashed potatoes
With gravy that was hot
And fresh-baked bread
Was not forgot.

Many a salad and
Vegetables galore
Greeted the crew,
As they came in the door.

When I was a girl,
Women didn't help with the branding
So while they all ate
I was left standing.

Women and girls
Were the last to eat,
When finally at the long table,
They got a seat.

Today there's the same work
For the ranch wife to do
But now girls are a part
Of the branding crew.

1-27-05

Fence-Building Day

There they stood—
All in a line.
This job of building
Was mighty fine.

He looked at his blisters
From using the diggers.
To hold the cows in
Was well worth it, he figures
.

He had dug the holes deep
Then the posts he set.
He tamped the dirt down
But still he did fret

Would this fence he was building
Hold out the bulls—
To keep them from the heifers
Were mainly his goals.

The barbed wire was stretched
And nailed to each post.
To build a strong fence
He wanted the most.

At last he was finished
And gave a loud sigh.
The fence he had built
Now was four wires high.

He then put the stretchers
And staples *away*.
He'd use them again
On another day.

He built this fence
By the sweat of his brow.
`Twas a thing of beauty
That caused no scowl.

Yes, he was tired
But well worth it, he'd say
For it was a successful
Fence building day.

10-9-01

[54] Nebraska Fence Post, July 29, 2002

My Trapper Dad

Out on the ice
My father did creep.
An appointment with destiny
He did keep.

You see, he was a trapper
Of muskrat skins.
The highest price for each pelt
He wanted to win.

He'd pound the steel stakes
Deep in the ice
To hold each trap
Each muskrat to entice.

He'd bait each trap
With fresh killed rabbit.
Carefulness in setting it
Was always his habit.

Then he'd leave
And go away
But he'd check each trap
Twice a day.

When a trapped animal
Was still alive,
It wasn't for long
That he'd survive.

Dad carried his rifle
Wherever he went
And in the head of the animal
A bullet was sent.

The animal was skinned out,
Stretched on a frame
And was there to dry
Until the buyer came.

The buyer always
Paid cash money
For pelts that you
Might think are funny.

Dad had coyotes and skunks
And civet cats too
Whose pelts the buyer bought
`Cause he wanted to.

Times were hard.
Times were bad.
'Twas how cash money was earned
By my trapper dad.

1-28-05

[55] The Fence Post, Plains Edition, March 19, 2005

Grandpa's Example

My grandpa was helping
Dad shingle our barn.
While he was doing it
He'd spin a yarn

Of how tough he was
And how he could eat nails.
The example of a grandpa
Never fails.

He put some nails in his mouth,
A handful you see,
And this was then
An example for me.

I remember the day
While in the swing
I put a nail in my mouth
Which was a very bad thing.

Before I knew it,
Out of the swing I had fallen
And I ran to the house
And began "bawling."

"I swallowed a nail,"
I said to my mother,
"To the doctor let's go,"
As she ran for my father.

So a hurried trip
We took to town.
"She did what?"
The doctor said with a frown.

A diet of bananas
I was placed on
Until the nail was passed
And until it was gone.

For ten days I ate
Only bananas each day
Until the roofing nail
Went its way.

Grandpas I warn you.
Be careful what you do
For some little child
May be following you.

4-11-05

[56] The Fence Post, Plains Edition, May 13, 2006

All Calls Must Go Through

Away out yonder
On a faraway hill,
Here comes the power wagon
Being driven by our Bill.

He took the power wagon
To help dig some holes
So he and his help
Could set some telephone poles.

Though he was tall and thin,
He had muscles that were steel
And he could handle by himself
Any old telephone reel.

If a line needed repair,
He'd strap his "climbers" on.
Up the pole he'd go
And it didn't take him long

To repair the needed line
So phone calls could go through.
He always seemed to know
Exactly what to do.

In the winter time
Bill would use a snowmobile
To go and check the lines
Which was sometimes an ordeal.

The snow would be quite deep
And he could hardly see.
To avoid hitting blowouts
He had no special key.

Sometimes he'd get stuck
And needed to winch himself out.
He had no one to help
For there was no one about.

A child might be ill
And a doctor might be needed.
A call to fix the phone
Our Bill always heeded.

Sometimes in the winter
Ice would build up on the lines.
Bill would go and fix them
Every single time.

Bill once in a while was known
For "burning a telephone pole,"
When his hooks came out
To just survive was his goal

Down the pole he'd slide so fast
That his clothes would be torn.
When each time this happened,
He never was forewarned.

One day when he was up
At the very top

A pole broke right in two
And Bill began to drop.

He hit the ground so hard
And on him the pole did fall.
He was in pain but amazed
His leg was not broken at all.

Every single holiday
Out on the line he had to go.
People needed their telephones,
 I want you to know.

Bill, as the telephone man,
Knew exactly what to do
And the standard that he lived by
Was — all calls must go through,

And they did thanks to Bill, the telephone man.

6-7-04

The Telephone Line

"Let's go and build a phone line,"
Bill said to Lloyd White.
It will be hard work
For it's got to be built right.

They loaded up some poles:
Twelve, eighteens and some twenties,
Creosoted treated poles,
All costing lots of money.

Wire, brackets, insulators,
Splints and tie wires
Were all needed for construction
Along with old car tires.

They headed for the Phiil Place
Where there was a great big hill.
To build a phone line over it
Would take all of their skill.

The south slope was too steep
So they approached it from the north.
When they achieved the summit,
The poles they brought forth.

And laid them on the ground
Where they could be worked on.
The brackets and the insulators
Were nailed where they belonged.

The poles were then carried
 Down the south side of the hill.
They had to be foot sure
So they wouldn't take a spill.

By hand the holes were dug
Three and a half to four feet deep.
These holes were spaced apart
About one hundred fifty feet.

Next the poles were set
And they were doing fine
While two high tension steel wires
Were strung along the line.

Next Bill and Lloyd rushed
To climb these telephone poles.
Hanging the wires on the brackets
Was their present goal.

At the end of the pole line
About a half a mile away
By means of a block and tackle
The wires were stretched that very day.

Tying the tie wires around
The insulators with a splint
Were accomplished with their hooks on
After climbing poles with backs unbent.

Bill and Lloyd White
Made hard work into a game

But that is when trouble
Almost to them came.

Remember they were building
Line down a steep, steep hill
And this was the game
That was played by Lloyd and Bill.

Bill would climb a pole
While Lloyd drove the pickup.
Bill would race to tie his wire
While Lloyd climbed the next pole up.

Bill would hurry down
And to the pickup he would run
To get to the next pole
While Lloyd had just begun.

They wanted to see who
Could get the most done.
That is where the trouble
For them had begun.

The last one in the pickup
Came upon a plan.
He'd take the pickup out of gear
And play catch me if you can.

Up and down the poles
Raced Lloyd White and Bill.
Remember they were building line
Down a steep, steep hill.

They'd run to the pickup.
One time it almost got away
For it was headed for a blowout
On that line building day.

Lloyd really laughed and laughed
At Bill as he ran
To catch that run away pickup
Traveling down that hill of sand.

Yes, those were the days
Before telephone buried cable.
To build the telephone lines
Took men who were strong and able.

Bill had many men
Who helped him and did fine.
Bill will always remember Lloyd and
The day they built that telephone line.

6-7-04

Cow Chips

On the Nebraska prairie
There was a need for fuel
For the winters there
Could be very cruel.

In the Sandhills
There were very few trees.
How did they keep warm
So they wouldn't freeze?

There was one fuel available
Just lying about.
It was the old cow chip
Though it had no clout.

I remember on the ranch
The process we did
To gather cow chips
Though I was a "kid."

We'd go to the windmills
Located on the range
Though you might think
We were mighty strange.

We took a hayrack
Or perhaps a wagon
And filled it with cow chips
`Til it was sagging.

With a purposed kick
I'd let my foot slip
Before I picked up
The nearest cow chip.

I'd not pick it up,
If it wasn't dry
And you now ask
Me why? Why? Why?

You see, a cow chip
Is nothing but manure,
I didn't want a wet one
You can be sure.

Outside our house
We'd make a high pile
Of dry cow chips
That would burn in style.

Cow chips, when burned,
Would produce great heat.
Carrying out the ashes
Made the routine complete.

Today this fuel
Would not make a hit
But I'm still thankful
For the old cow chip.

11-5-04

[57] The Fence Post, Plains Edition, February 5, 2005

Grandpa, the Marshal

My grandfather Vath
Was a big man.
Yet, he had a soft heart
Please understand.

Long ago
At Spotted Horse Hall
He was a man
That walked very tall.

You see he was assigned
To keep the order
`Cause people came
From all different borders

To drink and party
And perhaps to fight,
When a dance was held
`Till early daylight.

Grandpa, as a marshal,
Carried no gun
But carried a nightstick
In the place of one.

When alcohol got
The best of two men,
Usually an argument
And a fight would begin.

Grandpa would come
And break up the fight,
Which usually occurred
On a Saturday night.

Men respected my grandpa
Whenever he came near.
For the nightstick he carried
They had a healthy fear.

Those were the days,
When my grandpa walked tall,
When he was a marshal
At Spotted Horse Hall.

4-16-04

[58] The Fence Post, Plains Edition, June 24, 2006

Caught in the Snow

The snow was thick,
As it came down.
It covered everything
That was on the ground.

The wind picked up
And began to blow.
It fashioned drifts
Out of the snow.

I had on my face
A serious frown,
As I made my way
Home from town.

Would I get stuck
In some large drift?
From high to low
The gears I'd shift.

My pickup only
Crept along,
As I tried to keep
From doing wrong.

There was a steep hill
Dead ahead.
I should've added weight
To my pickup bed.

Almost when
I reached the top
And my pickup was
About to stop,

I prayed, dear Lord,
If you're not dead,
Please help me get up
This hill ahead.

I felt as though
Someone gave me a shove.
Did it really come
From God above?

I reached the top
And I was on my way,
I did not get stuck
Once that day,

My pickup didn't have
Four-wheel drive
But I made it home.
I did survive.

Whenever I climb
In my pickup to go,
I remember the day
I was caught in the snow.

I1-30-01

[59] Nebraska Fence Post, March 9, 2002

The Blizzard of 1949

What happened in January
Of "forty-nine"?
`Twas a horrible blizzard
Of the worst kind.

It was a Saturday
And we were in town,
When great big snowflakes
Began falling down.

"We're heading home,"
I heard Dad say.
"In Ogallala
We must not stay."

Thirty miles
We had to go,
As Dad drove home
In the blinding snow.

We made it home
All safe and sound.
Within a day
We were snowbound.

The cattle were in
Behind the barn.
They were all safe.
They'd suffer no harm.

Day after day
The snow came down,
Making drifts
That covered the ground.

In the midst of the storm
We heard a knock.
Two men came in.
For the doors weren't locked.

They'd got stuck
Just north of our trees.
It really is a wonder
They did not freeze.

The power was off.
We ate by lamplight.
When I looked out the window
It was a terrible sight.

I could see nothing but snow
So I ran upstairs.
The top of the snowbanks
Were standing there.

When it stopped snowing,
The work began.
Paths to the cellar
Were dug by hand.

As a child I was delighted
Because I could go

Over the clothesline
Which was covered with snow.

Someone came on a 'dozer
To get my Dad
Because of the experience
That he had.

Dad climbed on the bulldozer
And went away
To help dig out ranches
For he knew where they lay.

It seemed forever
Before Dad came back.
They also dozed out
Many a haystack.

It took forever
For this snow to melt.
I'll never forget
How this blizzard felt.

Nineteen forty-nine
Was a long time ago
But I'll always remember
That blizzard's snow.

12-3-02

[60] Nebraska Fence Post, January 18, 2003

The Cast-Iron Stove

There she stood
Against the wall.
For me, as a child,
She seemed quite tall.

She had in front
An oven door.
She had in back
A water reservoir.

She was black
With silver trim.
I still smell the bread
That was baked within.

A stovepipe went
To the chimney.
It carried the smoke out
From the stove, you see.

In the cast-iron stove
Mom would build a fire.
That it would heat quickly
Was her desire.

Two warming ovens
Were there on top
But the lower oven door
Was my favorite spot.

In the morning
On a cold winter day.
Let me get there first
Is what I'd pray.

The fuel we burned
Was dry cow chips.
At this city people
Would curl their lips.

They didn't understand
That we lived on the plain.
That gathering fuel
Was never a game.

The ashes in the stove
Had no end.
We took more out
Than the chips we put in.

In the summer it was hot,
As Mom cooked our meals.
 In the winter we loved
The heat we'd feel.

As modern days came,
We got rid of that stove.
It sat by itself
In our cottonwood grove.

In later days
She didn't survive,

`Cause we gave her away
To a cast-iron drive.

I have memories.
Yes, memories galore
Of the cast-iron stove
And it's oven door.

2-24-03

[61] The Fence Post, Plains Edition,
November 25, 2006

The Cream Separator

There she stood
In the middle of the floor.
She was about three paces
From either milk house door.

She had a hand crank
That protruded from her side.
A large bowl on top
Is where the milk did reside.

The crank was hard to turn
`Til you reached the right speed.
She was a cream separator
Of the sturdiest breed.

When reaching the right speed,
She literally would sing
And every turn you'd make
You'd also hear a cling.

On the front of the machine
She had two different spouts.
I watched as the cream
From one came pouring out.

It went into a bucket
On a table at its side
And my profound amazement
I never tried to hide.

Skim milk from the other
Flowed into a large pail.
You had to be careful
To put down the pail's bail,

Or milk would go a flying
And you would have a mess.
Sometimes I forgot.
This I must confess.

Our milk and cream today
Are bought in a store.
The need of a separator
Really is no more.

Like many other things
A cream separator's from the past
But my memories of her
Will always, always last.

10-23-02

[62] Nebraska. Fence Post, May 31, 2003

The Cellar

Into the cellar
I loved to go
And take my friends
Its bounty to show.

There were crocks of carrots
All filled with sand,
Placed there for eating
By Mother's hand.

There were sacks of potatoes
Picked up from the field
And brought to the cellar
From this year's yield.

There were jars of fruit,
Beans, tomatoes and more
That filled the shelves
That lined the floor.

The walls and roof
Were made of concrete.
You could stand up
But there was no seat.

The cellar was closed
By a heavy wooden door.
There were steps that went down
To the concrete floor.

There we kept the cream
In a ten-gallon can
To be shipped to town
By the rural mailman.

I remember the good smell
That was in the air
From the apples and vegetables
And cream that was there.

I remember a visitor
I hated to meet,
There in the cellar
Where he did creep.

Whenever I met him,
I would yell
And run to my mother
Who I would tell

"There's a visitor in the cellar.
Please bring the rake."
This unwelcome visitor
Was a dirty old snake.

This usually happened
Only twice a year
But when it did,
I was filled with fear.

Cellars are now
But a thing in the past

It's a memory of mine
That will always last.

12-31-01

[63] Nebraska Fence Post, November 9, 2002

Prairie Fires

Crash! Bang went the thunder.
Lightning streaked across the sky.
This was a thunderstorm.
The weather was hot and dry.

"I wish the rain would fall,"
A rancher said one night.
The thought of a dry storm
Filled everyone with fright.

The grass upon the hills
Had been dried by a wind.
The flashes of the lightning
Caused bumps upon one's skin.

The telephone did ring.
It gave a fire alert.
The rancher grabbed his pants
And quickly put on his shirt.

He quickly grabbed the sacks
And filled the water cans.
He also grabbed the shovels.
To the pickup the family ran.

The lightning struck nearby
And a prairie fire did blaze
On a neighbor's land
Where his cattle now did graze.

"God, please don't let the wind blow
Or this fire can't be stopped."
They all saw the fire,
When the hill they topped.

Women, men and boys
All worked side by side.
Dousing out the fire.
Their fear they didn't hide.

The smoke nearly choked them,
As they battled this prairie blaze.
They all worked with such fervor,
And were almost in a daze.

"It's heading for those buildings,"
Up the line went the cry.
When they thought they were defeated,
Rain came pouring from the sky.

Quickly the flames were doused,
As the rain came pouring down.
Some people had even come
From a nearby little town.

They were a tired, tired bunch,
As they headed home.
There's always a threat of fire
On the land where cattle roam.

Whenever I see a ranch
And wherever I see barbed wire,

1 always will remember
The threat of the prairie fire.

6-12-03

[64] Nebraska Fence Post, September 20, 2003

The Ride

Dad's combine and tractor
Sat next to the field.
It would determine
The amount of yield.

Dad asked me if I
Would go for a spin
Around the field
And back again.

I said "yes"
And climbed up the ladder.
What I wore
Really didn't matter.

I climbed in the bin.
It was neck high
And Dad began combining
The standing rye.

As the rye went in
The combine's belly,
It began to shake
Like a bowl full of jelly.

Out of the spout
And into the bin
The shelled out rye
Began pouring in.

I took my hand
Held it beneath the spout
And felt the grain,
As it poured out.

The grain was soon
Up to my knees.
I also tried
My knees to squeeze

But I was stuck
In just one place.
A few grains of rye
Even hit my face.

As the grain poured in
It came up to my waist.
I put some in my mouth.
It had a good taste.

Higher and higher
The bin was filled.
I was getting covered
By the harvest's yield.

Just when it came
Up to my chest,
The combine stopped
And took a rest.

A truck pulled up
Beneath the spout.

A trigger was released
And the rye poured out.

The bin was soon empty
And I climbed down.
I felt kind of shaky,
As I reached the ground.

I was covered all over
With wild sunflower resin.
It was hard to get off
Was one big lesson.

I enjoyed my ride
 In the grain bin
And I would do it
Again and again.

Combines of today
Are not pulled by a tractor
But are self-propelled.
An important factor

Though these grain bins aren't covered
No one can ride
For safety reasons
Access is denied.

One rides in a cab
Of combines today
But Dad combined
The old fashioned way.

Now I have shared
The experience I know
About my ride
Of so long ago.

2-22-02

[65] Nebraska Fence Post, August 14, 2004

The Pitcher Pump

Long ago we chose to move,
When I was only three.
The things that I remember
Are the things I did see.

The Rice Place that we moved to
Had a house two stories tall.
A pitcher pump in the kitchen
Is one thing I recall.

I really was amazed
We had water in the house.
I loved to pump the handle,
My little hands to douse.

The water was cool and clear
And it was sweet to taste.
I never again *was* scolded
For the water I did waste.

It used to be the bath water
Was carried from outdoors.
Now from the kitchen pump
Bathtubs were filled galore.

I remember the little squeak
The handle sometimes made,
When you pumped it up and down
And by its water you were paid.

A little time did pass
And remodeling was done.
The pitcher pump in the kitchen
Was replaced by a modern one.

The modern one was a faucet
With running water hot and cold.
 It was a sure replacement.
The pitcher pump was now quite old.

Yes, modern times had come
To our kitchen in the hills.
Modern faucets don't give you
The same sensation or the thrills

That water from a pitcher pump
Gives running on your hand.
If you had a pitcher pump,
You will understand.

Pitcher pumps now are gone.
They're an item from the past
But the memory of this three year old
Will always, always last.

6-12-03

[66] Nebraska Fence Post, June 12, 2004

Weeds for Dinner

Out in the prairie
There are good things to eat
Perhaps it's a weed
That's beneath your feet.

When I was a child,
To the prairie we'd go
Perhaps with a bucket
Or gunnysack in tow.

You see we were on
A mission that day
To gather lamb's quarters
Wherever they lay.

Lamb's quarters are
An edible green
And in the Sandhills
They're abundantly seen.

What would you do
With this weed growing wild
That I learned to recognize,
When I was a child?

We'd pick and carry them
Home that day
And wash them, then can them
In the regular way.

This weed tastes like spinach
And is delicious to eat.
When canned it makes
A winter time meal complete.

If you come to my house
In summer or winter,
You might find
We're having weeds for dinner.

7-29-05

[67] The Fence Post, Plains Edition,
September 3, 2005

Bibliography

[1] The Fence Post, Plains Edition, March 11, 2006

[2] The Fence Post, Plains Edition, September 24, 2005

[3] Nebraska Fence Post, February 7, 2004

[4] The Fence Post, Plains Edition, May 7, 2005

[5] Nebraska Fence Post, December 15, 2001

[6] The Fence Post, Plains Edition, April 1, 2006

[7] The Fence Post, Plains Edition, February 18, 2006

[8] Nebraska Fence Post, February 15, 2003

[9] Nebraska Fence Post, March 13, 2004

[10] Nebraska Fence Post, August 24, 2002

[11] The Fence Post, Plains Edition, January 13, 2007

[12] Nebraska Fence Post, November 22, 2003

[13] Nebraska Fence Post, July 26, 2003

[14] Nebraska Fence Post, March 15, 2003

[15] The Fence Post, Plains Edition, September 9, 2006

[16] The Fence Post, Plains Edition, March 10, 2007

[17] The Fence Post, Plains Edition, February 10, 2007

[18] The Fence Post, Plains Edition, November 12, 2005

[19] Nebraska Fence Post, September 28, 2002

[20] The Fence Post, Plains Edition, July 15, 2006

[21] Nebraska Fence Post, February 12, 2005

22 The Fence Post, Plains Edition, August 19, 2006

23 Nebraska Fence Post, April 5, 2003

24 Nebraska Fence Post, December 28, 2002

25 Nebraska Fence Post, October 25, 2003

26 Nebraska Fence Post, November 30, 2002

27 Nebraska Fence Post, July 20, 2002

28 Nebraska Fence Post, March 9, 2002

29 Nebraska Fence Post, January 25, 2003

30 Nebraska Fence Post, November 1, 2003

31 Nebraska Fence Post, August 7, 2004

32 Nebraska Fence Post, January 17, 2004

33 Nebraska Fence Post, August 17, 2002

34 The Fence Post, Plains Edition, October 21, 2006

35 Nebraska Fence Post, April 20, 2002

36 Nebraska Fence Post, September 1, 2001

37 Nebraska Fence Post, December 25, 2004

38 The Fence Post, Plains Edition, April 2, 2005

39 The Fence Post, Plains Edition, May 14, 2005

40 The Fence Post, Plains Edition, February 4, 2006

41 The Fence Post, Plains Edition, April 22, 2006

42 The Fence Post, Plains Edition, September 10, 2005

43 The Fence Post, Plains Edition, March 18, 2006

44 The Fence Post, Plains Edition, January 22, 2005

45 The Fence Post, Plains Edition, July 7, 2007

46 Nebraska Fence Post, November 10, 2001

47 The Fence Post, Plains Edition, May 27, 2006

48 Nebraska Rodeo Review, 2006

49 The Fence Post, Plains Edition, July 23, 2005

50 Nebraska Fence Post, September 25, 2004

51 Nebraska Fence Post, August 23, 2003

52 The Fence Post, Plains Edition, November 4, 2006

53 The Fence Post, Plains Edition, November 5, 2005

[54] Nebraska Fence Post, July 29, 2002

[55] The Fence Post, Plains Edition, March 19, 2005

[56] The Fence Post, Plains Edition, May 13, 2006

[57] The Fence Post, Plains Edition, February 5, 2005

[58] The Fence Post, Plains Edition, June 24, 2006

[59] Nebraska Fence Post, March 9, 2002

[60] Nebraska Fence Post, January 18, 2003

[61] The Fence Post, Plains Edition, November 25, 2006

[62] Nebraska Fence Post, May 31, 2003

[63] Nebraska Fence Post, November 9, 2002

[64] Nebraska Fence Post, September 20, 2003

[65] Nebraska Fence Post, August 14, 2004

[66] Nebraska Fence Post, June 12, 2004

[67] The Fence Post, Plains Edition, September 3, 2005

Endorsements

In the words of the old gospel hymn, "Precious Memories, how they linger, how they fill my soul with joy." Louise Hill has captured the memories of hundreds who've shared experience with her in the poems, *Daughter of the Sandhills*.

Louise has drawn us deeper into the mysteries of the "common experience": family, chores, games, school, work and our pets. In the sharing of these experiences there is understanding, healing, comfort, and peace; and above all a recognition of the goodness of God.
—Pastor Phil Ewert,
Retired

The poems Louise shares (with great detail) give us a peek into the "good old days." They reveal humor and fun in what others might say was such a hard way to live. Actually, we learn that having modern day pleasures does not guarantee us happiness and satisfaction in life. I find these poems most interesting and educational. My hope is that my children will read these poems to understand what previous generations went through to survive and sometimes thrive.
—Martin Flaming,
Agricultural Businessman

Daughter of the Sandhills will bring to life the experiences of those who were able to survive and thrive in the Sandhills of Arthur County, Nebraska. Through hard work, ingenuity and resourcefulness, the descendants of the pioneers were able to experience the satisfaction that comes from living close to the land and reaping the rewards that come from working the land.

Throughout this book of poetic reminiscence, the reader will note illustrations that portray clever inventions, the importance of community, family unity and a sometimes tenuous coexistence with wildlife. Those who experienced what it was like to grow up in the Sandhills will wax nostalgic as memories are stirred by A. Louise Hill's descriptions of times past. Others will gain an understanding of and an appreciation for the pioneer spirit.

It was my pleasure to depict these poems. Enjoy!
—Deborah L. Elkins,
Corporate Trainer

Daughter of the Sandhills is a remarkable poetic memoir depicting the pioneer life of A. Louise Hill and her family. By retracing memories of growing up in the "Western Sandhills" of Nebraska, Louise has poetically captured pioneer family life in the 1900's. Louise's poems paint portraits of pioneer times mostly forgotten and inventions of yesteryear.

Happily, A. Louise Hill's poems breathe life into the memories many of us have of "days gone by." Her poems depict a time when covered wagons rolled across the land. They describe the hardships of pioneer life, the use of water pumps, and the experiences of those taught in a one-room schoolhouse. Her memories of pioneer life include churning butter, milking cows, spring plowing, using cow chips, operating threshing machines, surviving the "Blizzard of '49," and many other enjoyable glimpses into pioneer history. Louise's poems capture memories of family life and reflect on growing up in Western Nebraska's Arthur County.

I am a teacher for the Ogallala Public Schools. Mrs. Hill has visited my classroom numerous times and shared her love of poetry with my students. She has always made the "pioneer lifestyle" come to life for my students by sharing her poetry. What a wonderful opportunity it has been for my students to hear Louise share poems about smelling skunk perfume, using cane fishing poles, sleeping with five kids in a bed, playing in tree houses, swimming in horse tanks, placing gum on the bedposts, riding bucking steers, listening to telephone party lines, and being scared by intruders in the outhouse.

It is an honor for my students to listen to a true professional poet read her poetry and discuss it with the class.

Readers will note that *Daughter of the Sandhills* is dedicated to Louise's loving husband, William B. Hill. We are all so blessed that Bill had a vision for Louise to complete this anthology of poems. They enable the reader to experience a "pioneer life" long forgotten. Louise, thank you for the many life lessons that you have shared with my colleagues, my students, and me!

—Taine J. Fruit,
Educator